Making a DIFFERENCE

Each of us is inspired by the lives of others.

SCHOLASTIC

LITERACY PLACE®

Copyright acknowledgments and credits appear on page 128, which constitutes an extension of this copyright page.

Copyright © 1996 by Scholastic Inc.   All rights reserved.   Printed in the U.S.A.
                                             ISBN 0-590-56635-0

                    5 6 7 8 9 10   24   02 01 00 99 98 97

Visit
a Concert Hall

Each of us is inspired by the lives of others.

Family Ties

We are inspired by the people closest to us.

Music Makers

We are inspired by artists and their work.

Everyday Heroes

We are inspired by everyday heroes.

Trade Books

The following books accompany this *Making a Difference* SourceBook.

Photo Biography

Anne Frank: Beyond the Diary

by Ruud van der Rol and Rian Verhoeven

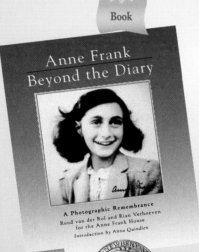

Fiction

Circle of Gold

by Candy Dawson Boyd

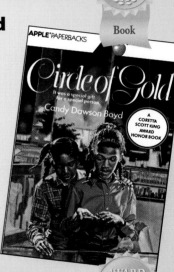

Newbery Award
Fiction

Dear Mr. Henshaw

by Beverly Cleary illustrated by Paul O. Zelinsky

Fiction

Racing the Sun

by Paul Pitts

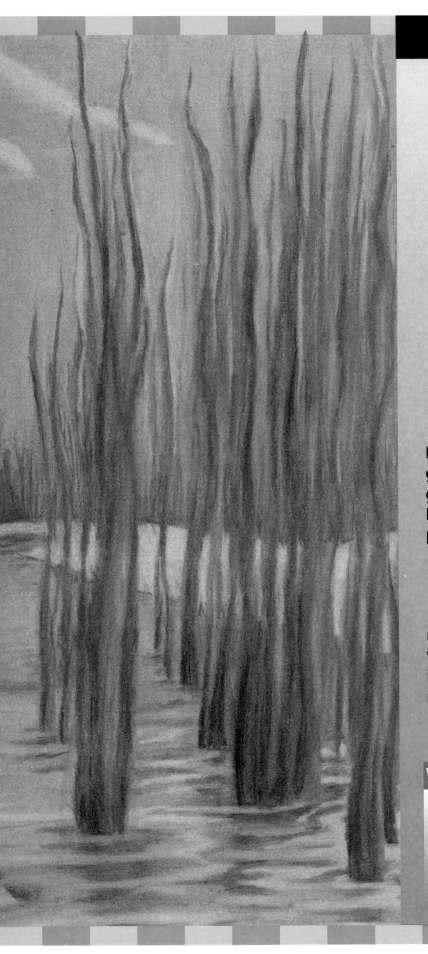

Family Ties

Find out how a young girl was inspired by her great-grandmother. Read another girl's poem about her family.

Meet Ken Griffey, Jr., who followed his father into the world of professional baseball.

WORKSHOP 1

Collect pictures, poems, and other items to create a montage of the people and things that inspire you.

9

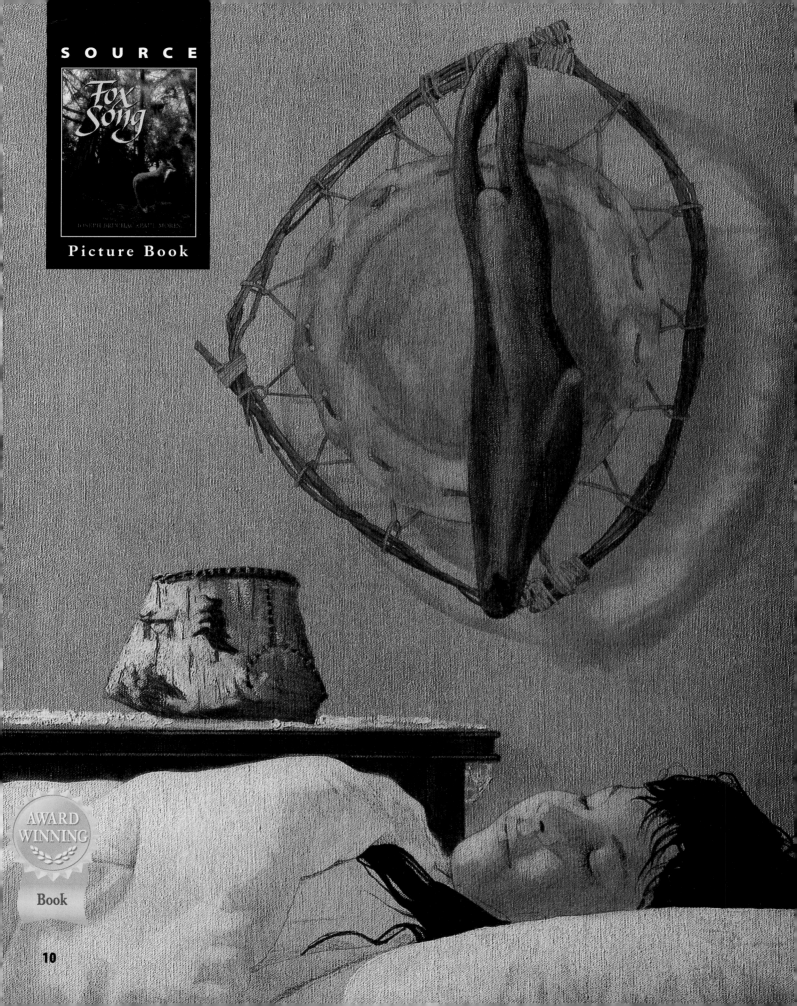

Fox Song

By JOSEPH BRUCHAC
ILLUSTRATED BY PAUL MORIN

The sun came slanting in through the window at the foot of Jamie's bed. She felt it on her face, but she didn't want to open her eyes. She knew what she would have to remember when she opened her eyes. She felt so alone. Perhaps now if she kept her eyes closed, she might be able to find her way back into the dream where Grama Bowman was with her.

There were so many things that she and Grama Bowman did together. It had been that way ever since Jamie could remember. Grama Bowman was actually her great-grandmother. She was Abenaki Indian and the mother of Jamie's mother's mother, and she was over ninety years old when she came to live with them in their house on the Winooski River, with the maple woods up the hill behind them. Such a long time ago, Jamie thought, six whole years. Most of my life. But not long enough. She kept her eyes closed, hearing Grama Bowman's voice telling her stories, seeing pictures in her mind of the things Grama Bowman and she loved to do together.

She saw them walking up Fox Hill in the heat of summer toward the slopes where the blackberries grew wild. Together they would pick out the berries that were, as Grama put it, "Just a little too ripe for us to take back, so we have to eat them here." Those berries were always the sweetest ones. Jamie remembered Grama explaining to her how their old people always cared for *alniminal,* the wild berries.

"They took care of them for hundreds of years before your father's people came here from France," Grama said. "Your father's people were good people. They learned from us that you have to burn off the dead bushes each year so that the new ones will be green and strong." Grama Bowman smiled. "His people were quick to learn, and we were ready to teach them. I think that is why we have kept on marrying them all these years." Jamie nodded and smiled, even though she was not quite sure what the joke was. She knew it was one of those things that Grama Bowman told her to hold on to and remember because the knowing of it would come to her when she was a little older.

The sun's warmth was even stronger on her face now. Jamie heard her mother come into the room and stand by the bed. Her shadow was cool across Jamie's face, but Jamie lay still, knowing her mother would not bother her. Her mother's soft steps went out of the room. Jamie looked for another memory and found them walking along the river until they came to the grove of birch trees. It was spring and the trees were green with buds.

Grama Bowman put her hand on the trunk of one of the trees. "You see this mark here?" she said, pointing to the shape on the bark that looked almost like a bird. "We Abenaki say this is the mark of Badogi, the Thunder. The lightning is his arrow and he shoots it during the storms. But he doesn't want to hurt our people and so he marked these trees. Lightning never strikes these birch trees, so if you have to be near any tree in a storm, better to be near a young birch tree."

Jamie looked up and nodded. "I understand, Grama."

Grama Bowman took some tobacco from her pouch and placed it near the base of the tree. "Brother, we are going to take some of your clothing," she said to the tree. "We thank you for this piece of your blanket." Grama Bowman smiled at Jamie. "You know, that is our Indian name for the birch. We call it *maskwa*, blanket tree." She took her knife and made a cut straight down the bark.

"We don't take too much so the tree won't die, Grama?"

"That is the way, Granddaughter, our old Indian way. Be careful what we take and only take what we need. Now," she said, "you help me pull. We must go this way, to the left. The same direction the sun goes around the sky."

The basket they had made that day, using spruce roots to sew it together after folding it and making holes with Grama Bowman's bone awl, was sitting on Jamie's table near her bed. She opened her eyes for a moment to look at it, and she could still see the patterns on the basket that her grandmother had made. The shapes of birds and ferns and animals. And her grandmother's bone awl was in that basket now. She hadn't understood why Grama Bowman had given it to her from her bag when she last saw her. Now she knew. She closed her eyes again, looking for her grandmother's face.

Grama Bowman's feet crunched through the snow in her white snow boots as they started on the trail to the maple grove up Fox Hill. Those boots were so big that the first time Jamie put them on—when she was a little girl—she couldn't move in them without falling. Grama Bowman always pretended that she couldn't remember which pair was hers and which was Jamie's. She would sit and struggle to put on Jamie's little galoshes while Jamie would stand in Grama's, giggling and saying, "Grama, I really think that these may be yours!" Finally they would have their galoshes on and they would finish the tea that Jamie's mother always insisted they drink before going out to check on the trees.

"Warm inside, warm outside," Jamie's mother said.

"You see, Granddaughter," Grama Bowman said, "that is the way the circle of life goes. You take care of your children when they are little ones and when you get old your children will take care of you. And they will tell you what to do, too!" The way she said it made everyone smile. Grama Bowman had a way of pursing up her face that would make her look like a little girl.

Then they went out into the late winter snow and up the trail toward the maple grove. All along the way Grama would point things out, the way the ice had formed on the twigs, the places where deer had browsed on the trees, the tracks of the animals. She loved to tell Jamie the stories those tracks told her. Listening to Grama's words, Jamie could see the animals as if they were still there.

"Old Owl, Kokohas, he dove down right there for Madegwas, the Rabbit," Grama said. "You see his wing marks on the snow? But Rabbit, he was too quick."

As they walked along, there was one set of tracks that Grama Bowman especially loved to see. "Look," she would say, "those are the prints of my best friend, Wokwses, the Fox. She is a clever one. I know her tracks well. Now she is out looking for her old man. She wants to have some little ones for the spring. Sometime," Grama Bowman said, "when you are out here and I am not with you, you keep your eyes open. You might see her and when you do, you will think of me."

Jamie nodded but she wasn't sure that she understood. She couldn't imagine being in the woods without Grama by her side.

It was another quarter of a mile beyond that clearing where they saw the tracks of the fox that they came to the line of trees that Jamie's father tapped for maple syrup. He would be along later in the morning with his tractor to collect the sap, but Grama always insisted that it was important for the two of them to come out whenever they could, just to make sure things were going right.

"We have to taste this sap and see that it is good," Grama Bowman said. She unhooked one of the buckets and tilted it so that Jamie could drink. There was nothing as light and subtly sweet as that taste.

Jamie opened her eyes and blinked away the tears. She closed her eyes again, afraid that she would no longer be able to see her grandmother in her memory.

But instead she found herself walking beside her along the hillslope. It was autumn, the leaves blowing in the wind, and it was very early in the morning. The sun was just coming up.

"My old Indian people," Grama Bowman said, "told me that the leaves love to dance. But they can only do their best dancing when they are ready to give themselves to the wind. That is when they are old, but they are the most beautiful then. They put on their best colors and then they dance."

A leaf came drifting past them and it brushed Jamie's face. It spiraled in the wind, went up and down, and then it touched the earth.

"When I see the leaves," Grama Bowman said, "I see my old people and remember they are still with me. We say that those who have gone are no further away from us than the leaves that have fallen."

The sun was a red arc lifting over the ridge and Grama reached out for Jamie's hand. "I brought you here to teach you a song. I forgot to teach it to my own daughter. But I know that you'll remember this song. It is a welcoming song and it says hello to the new day. It says hello to every new person you meet and it welcomes them. When you sing it, you will not be alone."

Grama Bowman began to tap her open palm on her leg as they sat there in the fallen leaves, facing the east. In a clear high voice she sang:

Hey, kwah nu deh
Hey, kwah nu deh, kwah nu deh
Hey, kwah nu deh
Hey, kwah nu deh, kwah nu deh
Hey, hey, kwah nu deh

She sang it twice and the second time she sang it, Jamie sang with her. By the time they finished, the sun was up and its warmth was on their faces.

Jamie opened her eyes and sat up. She felt the sun on her face and she got out of bed. She hadn't taken her clothes off from the night before, and her mother had come in and covered her as she lay on the bed. She went out of her room, past her grandmother's empty room. She went downstairs and walked through the kitchen. Her mother and father were there, but they said nothing to her. She loved them for that understanding. She took her light jacket from its peg near the back door and went outside.

As soon as she reached the path she began to run, her feet scattering the leaves that gleamed yellow and red in the October morning light. When she reached the slope that looked over their house toward the east, she leaned back against the same tree where Grama Bowman used to sit, and faced the sun. She took four deep breaths and the racing of her heart slowed. Then, still facing the sun, she began to sing:

Hey, kwah nu deh
Hey, kwah nu deh, kwah nu deh

Something moved at the edge of her vision and she turned her head slowly. A meadowlark came flying out of the bushes at the edge of the clearing. Then, a few steps behind it, a small dog came walking out. It stood perfectly still. Jamie saw it wasn't a dog at all, it was a fox. It was as if it was waiting for something. Jamie began to sing again:

Hey, kwah nu deh
Hey, kwah nu deh, kwah nu deh
Hey, kwah nu deh

The fox yawned and sat down on its haunches. The sunlight was bright on its coat and its eyes glistened. Jamie continued the song:

Hey, kwah nu deh
Hey, kwah nu deh, kwah nu deh
Hey, kwah nu deh
Hey, kwah nu deh, kwah nu deh
Hey, hey, kwah nu deh

Jamie finished the song and looked away from the fox. She closed her eyes, feeling the warmth of the sun, which touched her face and touched the earth. When she opened her eyes again, the fox was gone. Had it really been there? She didn't know, but as she rose and went back down the hill, she knew that she would never be alone.

GIFTS

by **Michelle Whatoname**

from **Rising Voices:**

Writings of Young Native Americans

Selected by

Arlene B. Hirschfelder

and **Beverly R. Singer**

This poem is by Michelle Whatoname, a Havasupai.
The "Supai" live at the bottom of the
Grand Canyon along the Colorado River.

My grandma gave
me her little
dress that she used

to wear when she was
little. My grandpa
gave me the part

of land that he
owned. My father
gave me his best horse

before he passed away.
Now I still have the
horse. Whenever I feed

or ride the horse, I think
of my father. When I
wear the dress my grandma

gave to me I think of
her. My grandpa gave me
part of his land. I always

clean and plant on it.
These things were blessed first.

THE MACMILLAN BOOK OF
BASEBALL
STORIES
by Terry Egan, Stan Friedmann, and Mike Levine

with an introduction by Tommy John

Sports
Anthology

AWARD
WINNING

Book

From The Macmillan Book of Baseball Stories
by *Terry Egan, Stan Friedmann & Mike Levine*

Like Father, Like Son:
the
GRIFFEYS

Ken Griffey, Sr., and his son Ken, Jr., played alongside one another for two years as Seattle Mariners. Even after Ken, Sr., retired from playing in 1991, he kept the father-son team together by becoming the Mariners' batting instructor. Here's how this story of family inspiration began.

On a chilly April morning in 1976, seven-year-old Ken Griffey, Jr., was playing catch with his dad.

"Hey, Pops, throw me some more grounders," said young Ken.

His dad, All Star outfielder for the world champion Cincinnati Reds, fired a hard bouncer to the boy's left. The boy lunged with his outstretched glove and snared it.

For millions of kids, the first day of a new baseball season is magical. Families everywhere rediscover the simple joy of playing catch, as generations share this springtime celebration on playing fields across America.

"Hey, that's not a bad catch, son," said Ken senior.

The boy couldn't hide his proud smile. "C'mon, Dad, throw me another."

The next grounder hit a pebble and took a bad bounce. Junior bobbled it once, picked it up, and dropped it àgain. He grabbed it once more but as he was about to throw, the ball slipped out of his hand and rolled down his arm.

Ken Griffey, Sr.

"Bet you can't do that again," joked his father.

They both nearly fell down laughing on the new grass. Dad had always told his boy that the best thing about playing baseball was having fun.

After a few more throws, Junior's mom, Birdie, called out into the backyard, "Time for breakfast, fellas." Father and son rushed inside, sweaty and dirty, still laughing about the muffed grounder. Dad and Birdie cooked up some eggs and toast for Junior and his little brother, Craig.

"Dad, can we go to the ballpark with you today?" asked Ken junior.

"If it's okay with Mom," said his father.

Mrs. Griffey smiled and said, "Well, I guess we could find our way out there."

Junior loved going out to Riverfront Stadium, where the Reds played. He'd watch the big crowd file in and listen to the vendors yelling, "Get your scorecard!" and smell the hot dogs sizzling on the

grill. He'd pound his glove hoping a foul ball would come his way.

This day, his dad invited him out to the field where the players were warming up. Again father and son played catch. Dad threw some grounders and the boy gobbled up nearly every one. Ken senior introduced his son to some of his Reds teammates—catcher Johnny Bench, first baseman Tony Perez, second baseman Joe Morgan.

"Hey, son," asked Perez, "you wanna be a ballplayer one day like your dad?"

Junior blushed. "Only if that's what he wants," said his father.

Many seasons passed. Father and son kept playing the game they loved. Dad continued to be a major league star. He traveled from town to town far away from home. Ken junior didn't get to play catch with his dad as much as he wanted. He missed him.

The boy rode his dirt bike and went skateboarding. To his mother's horror, he liked collecting worms and leaving them in his pockets. What he loved most, though, was playing baseball. He would throw the ball around with his younger brother, Craig. He played ball with Pete Rose's son, Pete junior, and with Tony Perez's kids, Victor and Eduardo. Ken's mom took him to play in the Little League games. He wished his father could watch him play, especially when he had a great game.

"Dad, guess what?" he shouted to his father over the phone. "I had three hits today."

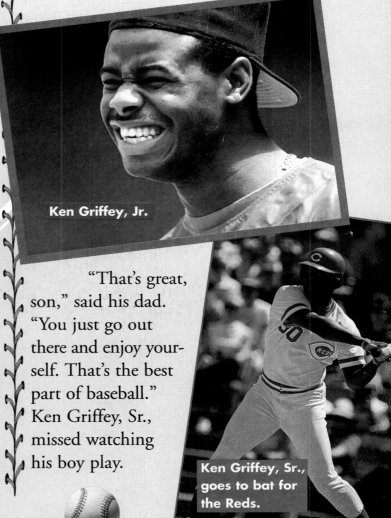

Ken Griffey, Jr.

"That's great, son," said his dad. "You just go out there and enjoy yourself. That's the best part of baseball." Ken Griffey, Sr., missed watching his boy play.

Ken Griffey, Sr., goes to bat for the Reds.

Ken Griffey, Jr.,
at the plate

The more baseball Ken junior played, the better he became. His left arm uncorked powerful throws. Soon he was belting baseballs over fences on high school fields. His brother, Craig, and his mom always came to watch him play. One day men with clipboards came to watch young Ken and take notes. They were major league scouts.

At the age of seventeen, Ken Griffey, Jr., signed with the Seattle Mariners. He went to play on the Mariners' Bellingham, Washington, farm team. He was away from home for the first time and he was a little scared. He missed his

Father and son

family. He just wanted to be in the backyard having a catch with his dad.

For the first time in his life, Ken junior stopped having fun playing baseball. He fell into a horrible slump, batting only .230. Everyone was on his case, even his dad. He felt like his father was looking at him as a ball player and not as a son. Finally, his mom came to visit. His dad, playing in Cincinnati, called again. He had thought it over.

"Son, I know what it's like being homesick. I miss you and mom and Craig a lot. We'll all be together soon. Now, don't worry about a thing. Just go out and enjoy yourself."

Ken took his dad's advice. The next day, the boy's season turned around. He began pounding the ball. By the end of the summer, his batting average zoomed one hundred points.

The next year, Ken Griffey, Jr., still only a teenager, made the big league club. He dazzled fans with his speed, his power, and most of all, his love of the game.

In 1990, young Ken got off to a great start, leading the American League in hitting.

His dad's Cincinnati Reds were on a roll, too. They talked often on the phone, sharing their good news. More than anything, the son wished his father could watch him play.

On April 26 Ken junior was standing in center field in Yankee Stadium. His Mariners were playing the Bronx Bombers. It was the bottom of the fourth. Yankee Jesse Barfield blasted a fastball into left center field, the deepest part of the stadium. Everyone in the ballpark thought it would be a home run.

Ken wouldn't give up. He raced back, legs churning, his eye on the ball. Back, back, back to the warning track. He dug his right cleat halfway up the eight-foot wall. He leaped. As the ball disappeared into the night, Griffey flung his arm over the center field fence.

When he came back down he held his glove high above his head. The ball was tucked safely in his mitt. Without breaking stride, he headed toward the Mariners' dugout, holding the final out of the inning.

At first the Yankee fans were silent in disbelief. Then they rose to their feet, thundering applause upon the young ballplayer from the opposing team. Ken junior broke into a big smile. He waved his glove at a distant figure in the stands. His father waved back.

The elder Griffey had flown to New York on his day off to see his son play. After the game, a mob of reporters gathered around Junior to ask about his spectacular catch. They were hanging on his every word. Here was a young sensation, hitting close to .400, stealing bases, banging home runs.

"What's your secret?" the writers asked Ken Griffey, Jr.

He shrugged his shoulders and said, "I guess I have fun playing baseball."

His father was standing in the locker room watching him. Junior looked up and saw his dad.

"Hey," Dad told his son, "that wasn't a bad…"

Nothing more was said. They stood there for a long moment and smiled at each other. That night they had dinner together. Then Dad had to catch a plane to rejoin the Reds.

"See you soon," said his dad.

Junior continued to star for the Mariners. He talked to his father on the telephone when they could. After one of those conversations, Ken Griffey, Sr., had an idea.

On the last day of August 1990, Ken junior trotted out to center field for the start of a game against the Kansas City Royals. Jogging alongside him was the left fielder. Ken junior felt a tingle of excitement down his back. The new left fielder was none other than his dad.

They were major league teammates. Ken senior had given up his chance to play on a championship team in order to play alongside his son. The crowd at the Seattle Kingdome let out a roar. This was the first time in history that a father and son had played on the same team. The two started warming up, throwing the ball back and forth. It seemed so familiar, yet so new. Ken junior looked up into the stands and saw his mom. The young man was so happy. I feel like crying, the center fielder thought to himself.

In the bottom of the first inning, the Mariners came up to bat. With one out, Ken senior stepped into the batter's box. On deck was Ken junior. A thought crossed his mind: Wouldn't it be great if Dad got on base and I was able to drive him home? He started laughing.

Suddenly Junior piped up, "Come on, Dad!"

Ken senior heard him. He began laughing so hard, he had to step out of the batter's box. He had never heard "Come on, Dad" before in the major leagues. No one had. Even the guys in the dugout were laughing.

Griffey stepped back in to hit, and Kansas City pitcher Storm

Ken Griffey, Jr., keeps his eye on the ball.

Davis threw him a fastball. He punched it past the second baseman for a single.

With his dad on first, Ken junior came up to bat. He lined a single to center, sending Dad to second. The bases were full of Griffeys. They both came around to score that inning as the Mariners breezed to a 5–2 victory.

Microphones and cameras surrounded the Griffeys in the clubhouse. And when later that month father and son hit back-to-back homers, they were the talk of America. The Griffeys were invited to appear on TV shows. President George Bush sent them a telegram of congratulations.

They were grateful for the honors they received and knew that in some way their lives had changed forever. They also realized that what was most important to them hadn't changed at all. Once again, father and son were playing catch, as they have throughout the years on fields across America.

A Closer Look

The Griffeys are a great father-son team, but how do they stack up as baseball players? The statistics below show each Griffey's performance after five years in the major leagues. How do father and son compare?

KEN GRIFFEY, SR.

Home Runs	37
RBI	273
Hits	783
Runs	456
Extra Base Hits	202
Batting Average	.286

KEN GRIFFEY, JR.

Home Runs	132
RBI	453
Hits	832
Runs	424
Extra Base Hits	317
Batting Average	.303

Stats compiled by Wayne Coffey
Sportswriter, *New York Daily News*

How to
Make a Montage

One way to tell others about yourself is to create a montage of the people, places, and things that inspire you.

What is a montage? A montage is a big picture made up of lots of smaller items, such as magazine pictures, newspaper clippings, drawings, or photos, pasted together. Usually all of the items in a montage relate to the same topic. Sometimes the items in a montage are put together to form a theme-related shape, such as a person, item, or scene.

Favorite songs, poems, or sayings—even an excerpt from a favorite book—are typical items in a montage.

Original artwork might be found in a montage.

This montage includes pictures of favorite places.

Items such as this one represent hobbies and special interests.

A montage might include photos of special people and animals.

1 Brainstorm

If you let people peek into your backpack, what would they see? Along with your homework, they might find items that tell about the people and things that inspire you. Brainstorm a list of inspirations you'd like to share.

Think of catgories —such as people, places, sports, hobbies, and pets— and come up with an item for each category. Single items may not mean much by themselves, but when you put them together, they tell about who you are.

TOOLS

- newspapers and magazines
- mementoes and souvenirs
- large envelope
- art supplies

2 Collect and Clip Items

Decide how you will represent your interests and inspirations in your montage. If you're including a favorite singer, you might copy down a few lyrics or use a CD cover. If you love the beach, you may want to use a shell or some sand. Clip words and pictures from old magazines and newspapers. Consider items such as letters, photos, drawings, sheet music, ticket stubs, and baseball cards. Make sure you don't cut up anything that you might want later. Keep your clipped items in an envelope so that you don't lose anything.

3 Create Your Montage

Gather all of your items, along with a piece of posterboard for mounting your montage. Decide how you want to form the montage. Before you glue your items, lay them out on the posterboard. You may want them to form a particular shape. Remember, too, that you can draw directly on the posterboard if you like. When you are happy with the form of your montage, glue the items to the posterboard.

Tip Treat your montage as though it were going to be exhibited in a museum. On a note card, write your name, the date you completed the montage, and a list of the materials you used. Hang the card next to your completed montage.

4 Share Your Montage

To prepare to share your montage with the class, give it a title. If you haven't already prepared a guide to accompany your work, write up a short description. In your description include a sentence or two about how each item inspires you. Hang your montage and present it to the class so others have an opportunity to get to know you better. You might want to give an informal talk about your montage, using your description as the base for the talk.

If You Are Using a Computer ...

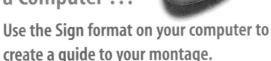

Use the Sign format on your computer to create a guide to your montage.

THINK

In making your montage, what did you learn about yourself and your inspirations?

Joseph Shabalala
Musician ▶

SECTION 2

We are inspired by artists and their work.

Music Makers

Read about music student Minna Pratt, who's inspired by a new boy in her class.

Meet ten-year-old trumpet player Josh Broder and some of the people who have inspired him.

Explore the music of South Africa with musician Joseph Shabalala.

WORKSHOP 2

Get the facts about an inspiring person, and write a biographical sketch.

AGE: 46 years old

DISABILITY: Paraplegic (17 years disabled). Paraplegia is a paralysis of the lower half of the body, including both legs.

COMPETITIONS: 100's. 9-time NYCM

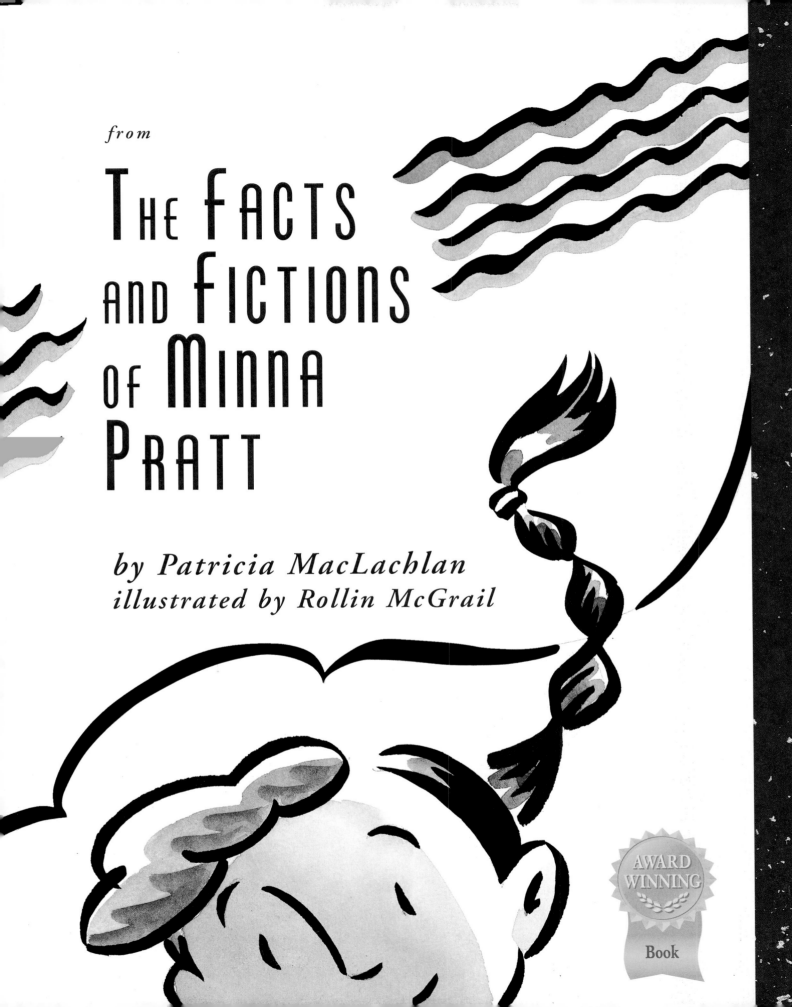

from

The Facts and Fictions of Minna Pratt

by Patricia MacLachlan
illustrated by Rollin McGrail

AWARD WINNING Book

elinda Pratt rides city bus number twelve to her cello lesson, wearing her mother's jean jacket and only one sock. Hallo, world, says Minna. Minna often addresses the world, sometimes silently, sometimes out loud. Bus number twelve is her favorite place for watching, inside and out. The bus passes cars and bicycles and people walking dogs. It passes store windows, and every so often Minna sees her face reflection, two dark eyes in a face as pale as a winter dawn. There are fourteen people on the bus today. Minna stands up to count them. She likes to count people, telephone poles, hats, umbrellas, and, lately, earrings. One girl, sitting directly in front of Minna, has seven earrings, five in one ear. She has wisps of dyed green hair that lie like forsythia buds against her neck.

There are, Minna knows, a king, a past president of the United States, and a beauty queen on the bus. Minna can tell by looking. The king yawns and scratches his ear with his little finger. Scratches, not picks. The beauty queen sleeps, her mouth open, her hair the color of tomatoes not yet ripe. The past president of the United States reads *Teen Love* and *Body Builder's Annual.*

Next to Minna, leaning against the seat, is her cello in its zippered canvas case. Next to her cello is her younger brother, McGrew, who is humming. McGrew always hums. Sometimes he hums sentences, though most often it comes out like singing.

McGrew's teachers do not enjoy McGrew answering questions in hums or song. Neither does the school principal, Mr. Ripley. McGrew spends lots of time sitting on the bench outside Mr. Ripley's office, humming.

Today McGrew is humming the newspaper. First the headlines, then the sports section, then the comics. McGrew only laughs at the headlines.

Minna smiles at her brother. He is small and stocky and compact like a suitcase. Minna loves him. McGrew always tells the truth, even when he shouldn't. He is kind. And he lends Minna money from the coffee jar he keeps beneath his mattress.

Minna looks out the bus window and thinks about her life. Her one life. She likes artichokes and blue fingernail polish and Mozart played too fast. She loves baseball, and the month of March because no one else much likes March, and every shade of brown she has ever seen. But this is only one life. Someday, she knows, she will have another life. A different one. A better one.

McGrew knows this, too. McGrew is ten years old. He knows nearly everything. He knows, for instance, that his older sister, Minna Pratt, age eleven, is sitting patiently next to her cello waiting to be a woman.

"Unclothed Woman Flees from Standard Poodle," sang McGrew, reading the headlines. "Boa Constrictor Lives in Nun's Sewing Basket. Sit down, Minna Pratt," he sang on.

"Hush up, McGrew," said Minna. "A mysterious woman just got on the bus. Number fifteen."

"Mysterious how?" sang McGrew, ending on a high note just above his range.

"A fur cape, gray braids, one earring," said Minna. "That makes seventeen earrings total on this bus."

"Emily Parmalee just got her ears pierced," said McGrew in his speaking voice. "She's meeting us at the bus stop."

Minna snorted, but not unkindly. Emily Parmalee was the catcher on McGrew's baseball team. She was, like McGrew, small and squat, with an odd sense of humor. Often she caused Minna to laugh so hard that she had to lie down on sidewalks or crouch in soda shops. Minna smiled, thinking enviously of Emily Parmalee, rushing toward womanhood faster than Minna, her ears already past puberty.

The bus jolted to a stop and Minna leaned her head against the window and thought about her lesson. Minna never practiced, except for the short times when everyone was out of the house. When no one was there, she could play bad notes without anyone calling out or McGrew humming them in tune as a guide. Minna never needed to practice, really.

She could, in the presence of her cello teacher, Mr. Porch, summon up the most glorious notes; pure, in fact, surprising even Minna. She played beautifully for Mr. Porch, mostly because she wanted to make him smile, as somber as he sometimes was. Also, she felt sorry about his name. Porch. Verandah might have been better. Or even Stoop. Porch was a dismal name. For a sometimes dismal man. McGrew called him Old Back.

Someone pulled the bell cord and it was their stop. McGrew folded his newspaper under his arm, reaching over to the seat across the aisle to snatch *The Inquirer*, forbidden at home even though it had the best headlines. Minna propped her cello on her hip and pushed through the crowd.

"Pardon. I'm sorry. Excuse."

The beauty queen woke up, closing her mouth and gathering packages. The past president of the United States put *Teen Love* and *Body Builder's Annual* carefully between the pages of his *Atlantic Monthly*. The king scratched on.

Emily Parmalee was at the bus stop with the shirt of her long underwear worn on the outside and brand-new holes in her ears.

"McGrew!"

"Emmy!"

They always greeted each other as if they had been lost on the prairie, smiles and exclamation points. A matched pair of luggage, thought Minna.

"Hallo, Emily," said Minna. "I like your ears."

Emily Parmalee grinned.

"I'll have feathers within the month," she said matter-of-factly.

Minna pulled her cello up the steps to the conservatory. The sky was gray, with low clouds, like in an old painting.

"I'll be forty-five minutes today, an hour at the most," Minna called.

"That's all Old Back can take," said McGrew, sitting down and taking a very black banana out of his jacket pocket.

On this dismal day Minna Pratt, cellist, climbs the steps to her dismal lesson with her sometimes dismal teacher, Porch. Outside sits McGrew with a dismal banana. And Emily Parmalee, who does not yet have feathers. Dismal is all Minna can think of. A dismal life. But she is wrong. Old Back Porch has a surprise for her. The surprise is not Mozart. The surprise is not dismal. It is Lucas, tall and homely and slim with corn-colored hair. With blue eyes, one that looks off a bit to the side. And with a wonderful vibrato.

inna paused before the great wooden door of the conservatory and looked up for good luck to where the gargoyles rested, gray and ominous and familiar. Then she pushed open the door and began the walk up the three flights of stairs. There was an elevator, but it was self-service, and Minna had nightmares of being stuck there between floors with no one to talk with, nothing to count. Alone with her cello. Minna, of course, would not practice.

TV Announcer: "After three days and two nights of being stranded in an elevator, Minna Booth Pratt has emerged, blinking and looking rested."

Minna: [Blinking and looking rested.]

TV Announcer: "A record, ladies and gentlemen! Seventy-two hours in an elevator without practicing!"

[Applause, applause, cheering.]

Sighing, Minna paused at the first-floor landing to look out the window. Below were McGrew and Emily Parmalee, slumped over like half-filled travel bags, singing. Minna pulled her jacket around her, the chill of the old building numbing her fingers. Far off she heard an oboe playing Ravel, a sound as sad and gray as the building.

She walked up the last flight of stairs, slowly, slowly, thinking of yesterday's lesson. It was Bartók, bowing hand for Bartók staccato; swift, short bows, Porch's hand on her elbow, forcing her wrist to do the work. When she got it right, he would smile his Bartók smile: there quickly, then gone. It would be early Haydn today. High third finger, she reminded herself, digging her thumbnail into the finger, forcing it to remember. After Haydn it would be the Mozart. *The Mozart. K. 157.* The number was etched on her mind, and Minna stopped suddenly, her breath caught in her throat. The Mozart with the terrible andante she couldn't play. The andante her fingers didn't know, *wouldn't* know. And then the wild presto that left her trembling.

Minna shook her head and walked on. Today was chamber group, three of them, with Porch, the fourth, playing the viola part. Called chamber group by all but Porch, who referred to it as "mass assembled sound."

Minna would be late. She was always the last one to arrive, no matter what early bus she took. Everyone would be there, Imelda and Porch; Orson Babbitt with his tight black curls and sly smile. Minna pushed the door open with one finger and they were tuning, Porch scuttling sideways like a crab between music stands with an armful of music. Imelda stopped playing and laid her violin on her lap, one foot crossed primly over the other, her black braids slick as snakes.

"It's three thirty-five," she announced, glancing at the clock. "And you've got only one sock."

"That's in case you care," said Orson, making Minna grin.

Rebarbative

Imelda was touched with perfect pitch as well as other annoyances. She pronounced varied facts even when not asked. She could recite the kings of England in order, backward and forward, the dates of major gang wars, important comets, what mixtures produced the color mauve. Imelda: fact gatherer, data harvester, bundler of useless news.

"It's WA today, Minna," called Orson from across the room, Orson's name for Wolfgang Amadeus Mozart. Orson played second violin with a sloppy serenity, rolling his eyes and sticking out his tongue, his bowing long and sweeping and beautiful even when out of tune. "If you must make a mistake," he had quoted, "make it a big one." Was it Heifetz who had said it? Perlman? Zukerman maybe?

"Tune, tune," said Porch briskly. He turned to Orson. "And is there a word for today?" Orson was the word person, spilling words out as if they were notes on a staff.

"Rebarbative," said Orson promptly. "Causing annoyance or irritation. Mozart's rebarbative music causes me to want to throw up."

Porch sighed. Orson preferred Schubert.

Suddenly Porch brightened, looking over Minna's head.

"Ah, good. I'd nearly forgotten. There is an addition to our group. A newcomer."

Everyone looked up. Minna turned.

"This is Lucas Ellerby," announced Porch, beckoning him in. "Lucas will play viola with us from now on."

The boy paused at the doorway. His hair fell over his forehead.

"Imelda and Orson," introduced Porch. "Minna Pratt, too."

Minna smiled. It sounded like the beginning of a nursery rhyme she half remembered:

Imelda and Orson and Minna Pratt, too,
Set out in a gleaming bright boat of blue....

"Lucas will play viola next to Minna," Porch went on. "I'll play first with Imelda. Trying hard not to be rebarbative."

Lucas smiled for the first time.

"That bad?" he asked.

Orson looked up quickly. There was a silence while Lucas unlocked his case and took out his viola and bow. Finally Imelda spoke.

"Have you heard the fact," she asked, her eyes bright, "that the great wall of China is actually visible from the moon?"

A fact, thought Minna. A mauve fact might follow.

Lucas sat down next to Minna.

"Yes," he said simply. He smiled a radiant sudden smile at Imelda as he tightened his bow. "Wonderful, yes? A fine fact."

inna watches Lucas's long fingers curl around his viola, one leg stretch out, one slide back to hook over a chair rung. There is a grand silence as they all stare at Lucas. Minna does not fall in love quickly. Most often she eases into love as she eases into a Bach cello suite, slowly and carefully, frowning all the while. She has been in love only once and a half. Once with Norbert with the violent smile who sells eggs from his truck. The half with one of her father's patients, a young man who made her breathless with his winks. When she discovered he also winked at her mother, father, McGrew, and the car, she slipped backward out of love again.

"Scales first," said Porch. "Old, familiar friends, scales. G to start."

They played scales, staring at nothing, no music needed because Porch was right . . . the scales were old friends.

"Now," said Porch, "let's begin with something we know. Mozart, K. 156. Presto, but not too presto." He raised his violin. "An A, everyone." They played an A, Orson making gagging noises.

Old Back lifted his bow.

The great wall of China, thought Minna. A fine fact.

"Ready," said Porch.

I wish I'd thought of that fine fact. Then Lucas would have smiled at me.

"Here we come, WA," said Orson softly.

"High third finger, Minna," whispered Porch.

nd they play. They begin together and Minna holds her breath. Often they stumble into the music, Porch louder, counting; Imelda scowling and playing too fast; Orson snorting in rhythm. But today is different. They begin on the same note and play together. In tune. Minna looks at Porch and sees that he has noticed the difference, too. Lucas's hand vibrates on the strings. They all hear the strong, rich sound of his vibrato. Lucas peers at Minna and grins. And suddenly Minna realizes that she is smiling. She has never smiled through an entire movement of WA Mozart. Ever.

"Splendid, splendid," said Porch, gathering up the music. Could they be finished already? One entire hour? "You are a fine addition, Lucas."

Imelda was smiling. Minna and Orson were smiling. Even Porch smiled.

"Tomorrow," instructed Porch, "the K. 157 andante. And the mimeographed variations. Practice! You, too," Porch said to Minna.

In the coatroom, Lucas locked up his viola. His jacket lay behind the case and he stepped around it carefully, gently picking it up, his hand covering the pocket.

Minna felt she must say something.

"You have," she began. She cleared her throat. "You have a wonderful vibrato."

Dumb, thought Minna with a sinking in her stomach. It was like saying that he had a lovely skin condition. Or both his legs ended nicely below his trousers.

Lucas nodded.

"I got it at music camp," he said solemnly. He looked apologetic, as if it might have been a mild case of measles, or worse, homesickness.

Lucas put on his jacket, then pulled a frog from the pocket. The frog was quiet and friendly looking.

"I saved him from the biology lab," explained Lucas. "I'm going to put him in the park pond. It's warm enough now." He looked at Minna. "Want to come?"

"Yes," said Minna quickly before he could change his mind.

Together they picked up their cases, Minna hoisting hers on her hip, Lucas's under his arm. In the hallway Lucas pushed the wall button, and it wasn't until the door opened and closed behind them that Minna realized she was in the elevator. The walls were gray with things scribbled there. The floor was littered with gum wrappers. There was a half-eaten apple in the corner.

The elevator started down, and Minna put out her hand to steady herself.

Lucas looked closely at her.

"Elevators can be scary," he said in a soft voice.

There was a terrible feeling in Minna's chest. The elevator seemed to drop too fast. There was a loud whooshing sound in her ears, and she looked at Lucas to see if he had heard it, too. But he was smiling at his frog. It was then that Minna knew about the sinking feeling and the noise in her head. It was not the elevator.

The door opened at the ground floor.

TV Announcer: "After three days and two nights, listeners in the vast audience, Melinda Booth Pratt is about to emerge from her elevator an accomplished cellist. With a vibrato. Accompanying her is Lucas Ellerby. Food and drink have been lowered to them, along with cello music. And flies for their frog."

Outside there was a slight breeze. McGrew and Emily were still sitting on the stone steps.

"This is Lucas," said Minna. "My brother, McGrew, and his friend Emily Parmalee, a catcher."

Lucas smiled. McGrew smiled. *All this smiling.* Emily Parmalee turned one earring around and around in her ear thoughtfully.

"We're going to put Lucas's frog in the park pond before the bus comes," said Minna.

Behind them the street musicians were beginning to play: a flute on the far corner, Willie, tall and bearded, by the steps playing Vivaldi in the dusk. Willie was Minna's favorite, playing whatever she wanted on his violin, giving her back her money.

They walk down the street, Minna and Lucas with two instruments and a frog between them, McGrew and Emily Parmalee behind, shuffling their feet. The street is crowded but strangely hushed except for the swish sound of cars passing cars. Lucas says nothing. Minna says nothing. Only McGrew breaks the silence.

"Love," he sings softly in a high thin voice behind Minna.

From A Very Young

Josh Broder was inspired to make music by many influences in his life. He has taken private lessons and studied music in school. During the summer, he sharpens his trumpet-playing skills at a sleep-away camp, Interlochen, in Michigan, where he studies with his instructor.

Once a week, after lunch, I have a private lesson with Craig Davis. On the days I don't have lessons, I practice.

It's very important to keep my instrument clean. It's dark inside the trumpet, and the dampness from my breath makes it easy for mold to grow there. I wash my trumpet out about once a month; and every day that I play, I begin by removing the valves and oiling them one at a time. Then I clean and oil the main tuning slide and adjust it so I'll be in tune when I play with other people.

There are many different techniques that go into playing the trumpet. Sometimes Craig and I start our lesson with mouthpiece buzzing. It's called "buzzing" because that's what it sounds like when you vibrate your lips against the mouthpiece. It takes a little more endurance to get a good buzz on the mouthpiece when it's not attached to the trumpet. That's because the trumpet is like a loudspeaker, and it amplifies the sound.

Musician
by *Jill Krementz*

Mouthpiece buzzing makes your lips stronger. This helps develop "embouchure," which means how you shape your lips and tongue when you blow into the mouthpiece. Most jazz musicians refer to embouchure as "chops."

Craig shows me how to finger the valves that control the pitches of the trumpet. The valves are on top, and I move them with fingers that are held firm. There are seven possible fingering combinations on the trumpet. That means you can play a lot of different notes. But you also have to think about the sound and the speed of each note. You have to coordinate how you blow into the mouthpiece and how you finger the valves to get just the right effect.

Craig tells me how important it is to fill up my horn. After I've warmed up, he says, "Now we're going to see how long you can tongue one note." He reminds me to keep the air moving through my instrument as I play lip slurs—that's when you go from one note to another note without pressing any valves.

Lip slurs are exercises that build endurance, range, and lip flexibility, and develop breath support.

I don't spend the whole day practicing or playing. In the afternoons, I take a nature course called Environmental Exploration. We go river wading, watch movies, and sometimes find wonderful Indian arrowheads and old pieces of pottery. Our camp is on Duck Lake, so we also do a lot of swimming.

At the end of the day, I usually jam with my friends Jeff and Louis. We play jazz to a background tape of percussion, bass, and piano. Jamming is a lot of fun, and quite a bit different from playing in a band or an orchestra. You don't always have to stick to the notes. You can improvise and express yourself by playing the music in different ways. You're playing together as a group, but you always have a chance to show what you can really do. Jeff, Louis, and I get along great; and I figure we'll probably be friends for the rest of our lives.

At Interlochen, the students who are studying dance put on ballet recitals and the drama students put on plays. The artists exhibit their crafts and paintings, and sometimes they even exhibit themselves.

We all have a chance to see these performances. We also have the opportunity to show off what we've learned. For me, that's one of the things that makes camp so much fun.

All summer long we have famous performers who hold master classes for the students and who perform in the evenings. This year Itzhak Perlman and Billy Taylor—two of my favorites—were guest artists. Itzhak Perlman played a violin concerto with the camp's World Youth Symphony Orchestra. Billy Taylor played piano with his trio.

When I got home from camp, my mom and dad took me to a Wynton Marsalis concert on Long Island to celebrate my eleventh birthday. He's one of my favorite musicians so this was a special treat. The concert was at a club called Wings. Since I usually set up the sound system for my brother's performances, I knew Wynton would probably be there an hour or two before the concert for a sound check. So I went early; hoping to meet him. Was I ever lucky! He did arrive early, and since I was the only one there, besides the waiters, I sat and watched him while he and the rest of his ensemble rehearsed.

Wynton Marsalis is not only a great trumpet player, he's also a great musician. He can play anything from classical concertos to modern jazz. He asked me if I had brought along my horn. I had, and he asked me to play for him. I was scared to death, but I played my long tones and some slur exercises.

Then he played his trumpet. He put my hand on his windpipe so he could demonstrate deep breathing—using a lot of air when you're playing—which is essential to trumpet playing. He told me how important it is to practice, to relax when I play, and to be humble. He said I should work on my scales; make every exercise musical; practice every day; and when I'm practicing to concentrate on every detail—to always know the reason why I'm practicing something. If I do all these things, he said, I'll be really good.

Wynton started playing when he was six and practicing seriously when he was twelve. His brother, Branford, is a great musician, too. Besides playing tenor saxophone, Branford has acted in quite a few movies. They both learned a lot from their father, who is head of the jazz department at the University of New Orleans.

At the end of the lesson, Wynton told me that I should always help other musicians and practice every day—he said that it shows in your tone.

While we waited for his concert to begin, I told my mom and dad that I would remember this birthday until I was a hundred years old.

The concert was wonderful! Wynton and the ensemble played "The New Orleans Function," which is a favorite of mine. It's one of the pieces from his album called "Majesty of the Blues." Between each set, he talked to the audience about the growth and history of jazz.

It's hard to believe that he's only twenty-seven years old. He's won eight Grammies, and he's the only musician who has ever won a Grammy for both jazz and classical music in the same year.

During the concert, I tried to imagine what it would be like if that was me up there. Wynton made it look so easy, but I know that hours and hours of practice go into every piece. I could tell that he loves music and loves to play for people.

Meeting Wynton Marsalis and getting to play for him was one of the most exciting things that ever happened to me. I still haven't decided if I want to be a full-time trumpet player when I grow up. I know I have a lot to learn. For now, I just want to be a better musician. But if I do stay with serious playing, I hope I'll always be as nice to young musicians as Wynton was to me.

Joseph Shabalala

Musician

Joseph Shabalala inspires *his fellow* singers.

Led by Joseph Shabalala, the singing group Ladysmith Black Mambazo performed on Broadway, toured the world, and won a Grammy Award. But singing is not all fun and games for Shabalala—it has a much deeper meaning. Joseph Shabalala's goal is to pass on his country's culture and traditions through his songs.

PROFILE

Name:
Joseph Shabalala

Job:
leader of Ladysmith Black Mambazo, a South African singing group

Favorite things to sing about:
hope and peace

Career highlights:
singing with Paul Simon, winning a Grammy Award, appearing on *Sesame Street*

Favorite thing to do when not singing: spending time with his nine children and four grandchildren

MORE ABOUT
Joseph Shabalala

Find out how *this musician* is inspired by his ancestors.

Returning to Roots

Ladysmith Black Mambazo is an *a cappella* singing group. They sing without instrumental accompaniment. The ten members of the group sing together in such perfect harmony that their voices become the instruments.

Joseph Shabalala was inspired by the work of a great Zulu tribal leader, Shaka Zulu. "Ladysmith Black Mambazo's music originated from Zulu songs and dances," Joseph Shabalala explains. "Shaka Zulu was a great warrior, but he was also an incredible dancer," he says. Shabalala and his group use a lot of traditional Zulu dance steps when they perform.

As leader of the group, it is Joseph Shabalala's mission to preserve his cultural heritage. "It's time to follow the footsteps of our ancestors," he says. "That's the only way to know ourselves."

Passing on the Music

How does Joseph Shabalala create his songs? "Sometimes I dream a song at night," he says. "Sometimes it's only the harmony. Sometimes I dream only the words." But whatever part Shabalala dreams, it's hard work putting the whole song together. It is important to him that his songs have meaning. Two themes that run through many of Shabalala's songs are hope and peace. "My music is about peace. It is about forgiving each other," he explains.

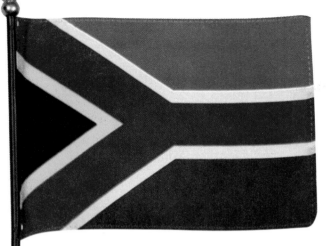

After Shabalala composes a song, he teaches it to his sons. "My sons are great singers and dancers," Shabalala says. "They are even better than I am." They are so good, in fact, that three of his sons are members of his group. But Shabalala doesn't just teach his sons how to sing and dance—he teaches them about their culture and the importance of preserving it.

Looking Toward the Future

Joseph Shabalala is also trying to preserve South African traditions for future generations. His goal is to open the Mambazo Academy of South African Music and Culture. Besides teaching basic academics, the school would teach children traditional music, dance, and customs.

Shabalala hopes that his music will inspire others to remember their roots. "I want to give the message," he says, "to be proud of who you are."

Joseph Shabalala's Tips for Young People of All Cultures

1 Talk to your parents. They may be able to tell you something about your heritage.

2 Write down what you learn. You might want to write a poem, a story, or even a song inspired by your cultural traditions.

3 Share what you've learned. Tell others who you are—and don't forget to listen to them, too!

How to
Compile a Biographical Sketch

When a person's accomplishments have been truly inspirational, the world should know all about him or her. Compiling a biographical sketch is a good way to share information about an important person.

What is a biographical sketch? A biographical sketch is a way of giving basic information about someone's life. This information includes facts such as where the subject was born and what special talents he or she has.

Basic information about a person is generally provided.

A profile highlights the characteristics that make a person famous, memorable, inspiring, or unique.

A photo of the subject adds interest.

ROBERT NEUMAYER

AGE: 46 years old

DISABILITY: Parapleg[ic] [(physically disabled). Paraplegia is [paralysis of] the lower half of the b[ody, including] both legs.

COMPETITIONS: 100's. 9-time NYCM competitor. Achilles member since 1986.

Robert won the NYCM (handicapped runners class) in 1989 and again in 1990. He has acted as a safety and health consultant for the Board of Education, New York Telephone and the Hilton Corporation. Robert has also spoken at over 300 schools.

Achilles Track Club

1 Choose a Subject

Think about someone who inspires you. What contributions has that person made to a profession, a sport, a country, or to your life? The person you choose can be a celebrity, your best friend, or a relative. In choosing a person, you might also consider the availability of information about that person. Will you be able to locate enough information?

TOOLS

- paper and pencil
- articles and books
- tape recorder (optional)

Tip What is your favorite thing to do? Do you like to go to the movies, play sports, or draw? Think about doing a sketch of the person who got you interested in this activity, or of a person you've discovered through a favorite activity.

2 Plan Your Sketch

Now decide what sort of details you would like to include in your biographical sketch. The information should be brief and to the point. Choose things to find out about your subject that match that person's job or interests. For example, if you've picked an artist, you might want to describe your subject's work and find out which artists inspire him or her. Make a list of all the things you want to find out.

3 Research Your Subject

If the person you chose is someone you know, you should be able to get all of the information you need by talking to your subject or to someone who knows your subject well. If the person is someone you don't know personally, look for information in magazines and newspapers, as well as in biographies or other books. If you can't find all the information you need in one place, check another source. Don't forget to take notes on your research. If you're conducting an interview with your subject, you might want to tape-record it. Find a photo of your subject to accompany the information you collect.

4 Complete Your Sketch

Use your notes or tape to help you decide which information to include in your sketch. Organize the information under headings like "Job," "Pets," and "Hobbies" and write a short entry for each heading. Try to include some unusual facts or particularly interesting information about your subject. If possible, attach a photo or drawing of the subject to the sketch.

Present your biographical sketch to your classmates. Include a brief oral or written explanation of how your subject inspires you.

If You Are Using a Computer ...

Draft your biographical sketch, using the Report format. If you like, you can keep track of your sources by using the Bibliography Maker.

THINK

If someone were writing a biographical sketch about you, what kind of information would he or she include?

Joseph Shabalala
Musician
▶

Everyday Heroes

Find out how an ordinary kid becomes an everyday hero. Meet real kids who are heroes in their own way.

Witness the courage of a girl who saves her friend from Nazi soldiers. Examine a poster commemorating heroes of the Holocaust.

P R O J E C T

Thank an everyday hero—or someone else in your life—by writing a tribute.

Jane Goodall

79

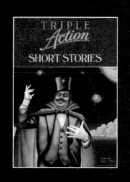
from
Triple Action Short Stories

Just a PIGEON

BY DENNIS BRINDELL FRADIN

ILLUSTRATED BY FLOYD COOPER

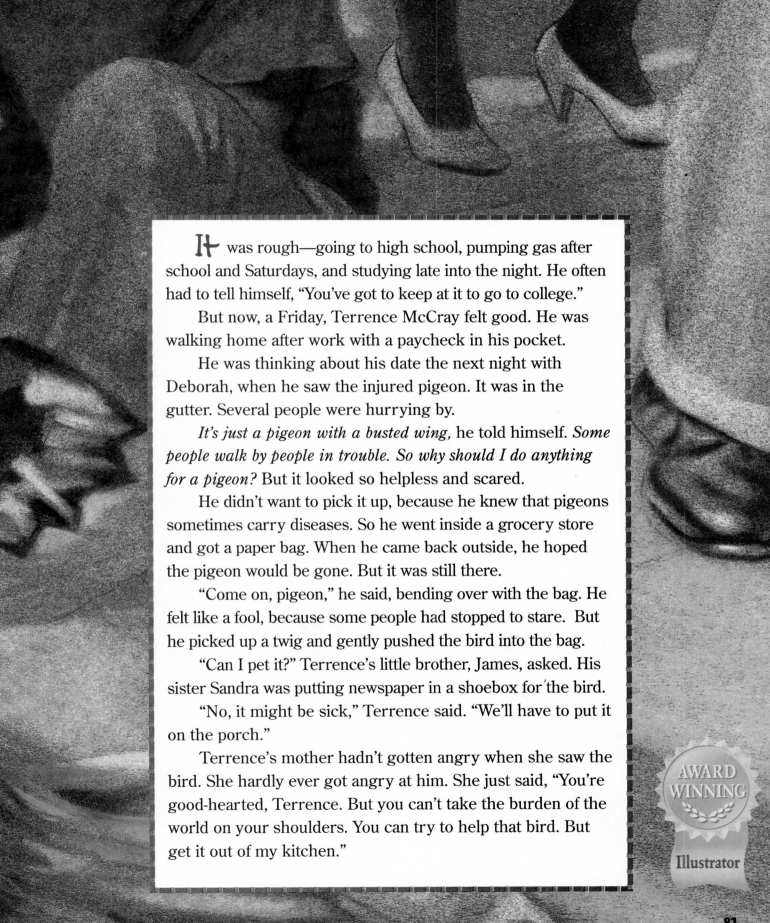

It was rough—going to high school, pumping gas after school and Saturdays, and studying late into the night. He often had to tell himself, "You've got to keep at it to go to college."

But now, a Friday, Terrence McCray felt good. He was walking home after work with a paycheck in his pocket.

He was thinking about his date the next night with Deborah, when he saw the injured pigeon. It was in the gutter. Several people were hurrying by.

It's just a pigeon with a busted wing, he told himself. *Some people walk by people in trouble. So why should I do anything for a pigeon?* But it looked so helpless and scared.

He didn't want to pick it up, because he knew that pigeons sometimes carry diseases. So he went inside a grocery store and got a paper bag. When he came back outside, he hoped the pigeon would be gone. But it was still there.

"Come on, pigeon," he said, bending over with the bag. He felt like a fool, because some people had stopped to stare. But he picked up a twig and gently pushed the bird into the bag.

"Can I pet it?" Terrence's little brother, James, asked. His sister Sandra was putting newspaper in a shoebox for the bird.

"No, it might be sick," Terrence said. "We'll have to put it on the porch."

Terrence's mother hadn't gotten angry when she saw the bird. She hardly ever got angry at him. She just said, "You're good-hearted, Terrence. But you can't take the burden of the world on your shoulders. You can try to help that bird. But get it out of my kitchen."

AWARD WINNING

Illustrator

After dinner, his mother got ready for work. Terrence rushed out and bought some birdseed.

When he got back, his mother was in her nurse's uniform. She said, "You brought the bird here. So you decide what to do with it."

While Sandra and James watched, Terrence fed the pigeon. Then he put the bird in the shoebox out on the porch.

Later, he could hear the bird cooing sadly. "Maybe I should have left it in the street," he said to himself. "It will probably die anyway."

On Monday, between classes, Terrence went to a pay phone. He looked up "Veterinarians" in the phone book, and dialed a number.

"Pigeon?" the doctor said. "Broken wing? I could try to fix it."

"How much will it cost?" Terrence asked.

"I couldn't tell. It could be expensive. If I can fix the wing, the bird will have to stay here a while. But you wouldn't have to pay me all at once."

After history class, Willie Barnes asked Terrence to shoot baskets in the gym.

"I can't, Willie," he said. "See, I found this pigeon with a busted wing. I've got to take it to the vet before work."

"What?" Willie said. "Spending money on a pigeon?"

Thad Lanier had stopped to listen. He stared at Terrence and said, "So many people needing help. And you spend money on a pigeon?"

"I saw it in a gutter," Terrence tried to explain. "I couldn't help it."

But Thad had turned and walked off with Willie, shaking his head.

Terrence took the pigeon to the vet. Dr. Landis said, "I've got to admit, this is my first pigeon. But I think I can fix its wing. Give me a call tomorrow."

The next day, Terrence called Dr. Landis. He learned that the bird's wing had been set, and it was doing well. When he told Sandra and James, they wanted to visit it.

"Tell you what," Terrence said. "When we let it go, you can come and watch. How's that?"

Terrence was glad about the bird. But he was worried about the money. Besides that, Thad kept making remarks. One afternoon, just before history class started, Thad went too far.

"Talk about your future black leaders!" Thad said. "How about Terrence here? He's spending his money on a pigeon."

"A what?" Deborah asked. "Terrence, is that why we couldn't go to the movies?"

"Yeah," Thad said. "He found a sick pigeon, and he's paying for it to get well. Meanwhile, poor people don't have enough to eat." Excited by his own voice, Thad added, "Hey, who's the pigeon?"

Terrence got out of his seat and rushed at Thad. Just then, the teacher walked in. Terrence didn't care. He raised his fist. But as he saw Thad's frightened face, he felt sorry for him. He also knew why he had saved the pigeon.

"It was in trouble," he said. "It was alive, like us. If you walk past an animal, next thing you might walk past a person."

"What's all this?" the teacher asked.

"Nothing," Terrence said.

Terrence took Sandra and James with him when he went back to the vet. He had plenty of money with him. But he kept hoping that somehow Dr. Landis would say, "Since you're so kind, you don't have to pay."

Dr. Landis took them back to where the animals were kept in cages. There was the pigeon, looking as healthy as any pigeon.

Dr. Landis took it out of the cage. Then they all went out through the back door, and Dr. Landis set the pigeon down gently on the ground.

"Good-bye, pigeon," James said.

Terrence half expected the pigeon to thank them somehow. But it just fluttered its wings and flew up to a window ledge.

Terrence reached for his wallet.

"That will be twenty dollars," Dr. Landis said.

Terrence counted out the money. Then he looked for the pigeon. But it had flown out of sight.

"Come on," he said to James and Sandra. He had to be at work in 15 minutes.

Just do it!

(These Kids Did)

Tree-mendous: Chase's planting program for kids spread from Utah to the nation.

Teamwork: Students at Gulf Beaches Elementary School in Florida created a natural habitat.

There are plenty of things kids like you can do in your homes, schools, neighborhoods, and communities to help preserve resources and clean up the earth. Here are just a few examples of kids who decided to become active and, each in his or her own way, made a difference.

Audrey Chase, 13
Menan, Idaho
Audrey, founder of Leaf It To Us, raised funds to plant more than 100 trees in Utah and successfully lobbied the state legislature for a tree fund for kids, which matches the money the kids raise. Then Audrey successfully lobbied for a similar national tree fund for kids.

Gulf Beaches
Elementary School
St. Petersburg, Florida
Working with the PTA and the local native-plant society, these budding naturalists have created a butterfly habitat and a maritime forest with native plants that need no pesticides and provide food and shelter for wildlife.

Leigh-Leigh Bradford, 12
Wheaton, Maryland
When Leigh-Leigh was 8, she decided to learn organic gardening. After successfully growing vegetables without pesticides in her own garden, she helped her grandfather write a book called "A Child's Organic Garden: Grow Your Own Delicious Nutritious Foods."

(Opposite) Healthy eats: Leigh-Leigh Bradford grows veggies organically.

Solar power: Wong designed
a prize-winning eco-car.

He's no dummy: Terry saves
sea turtles in Mexico.

William Wong, 11
San Francisco, California

Upset by the bus pollution in his city, William learned about solar power at school and entered the first Young Eco Inventors Contest with an idea for a solar-powered car. He won first junior prize in San Francisco last September. The contest will be repeated this year in Los Angeles.

Brady Landon Mann, 11
Vancouver, Washington

While in the third grade, Brady persuaded his school to start recycling classroom paper and milk cartons. Next, Brady helped persuade his city's curb-side recycling company to collect from apartments as well as houses. Brady also set up a program for neighborhood kids to pick up trash around their buildings for a dollar a bag.

Macon Terry, 12
Houston, Texas

In 1991, Macon made his first trip to Mexico to help endangered sea turtles. By last year, 67 Boy Scouts had made the annual trek to the Yucatán. Macon also enjoys using ventriloquism as a fun way to spread environmental messages.

Melissa Poe, 13
Nashville, Tennessee

When she was 9, Melissa Poe wrote a letter to President Bush asking him to save the environment. She got a form letter back. Instead of getting mad, Melissa got active. Today she heads a nationwide, 100,000-member organization called Kids For A Clean Environment (F.A.C.E.), whose

F.A.C.E. it: Poe started Kids
For A Clean Environment.

activities include planting trees and producing music videos about ecology.

Super recycler: Mann has
everyone picking up.

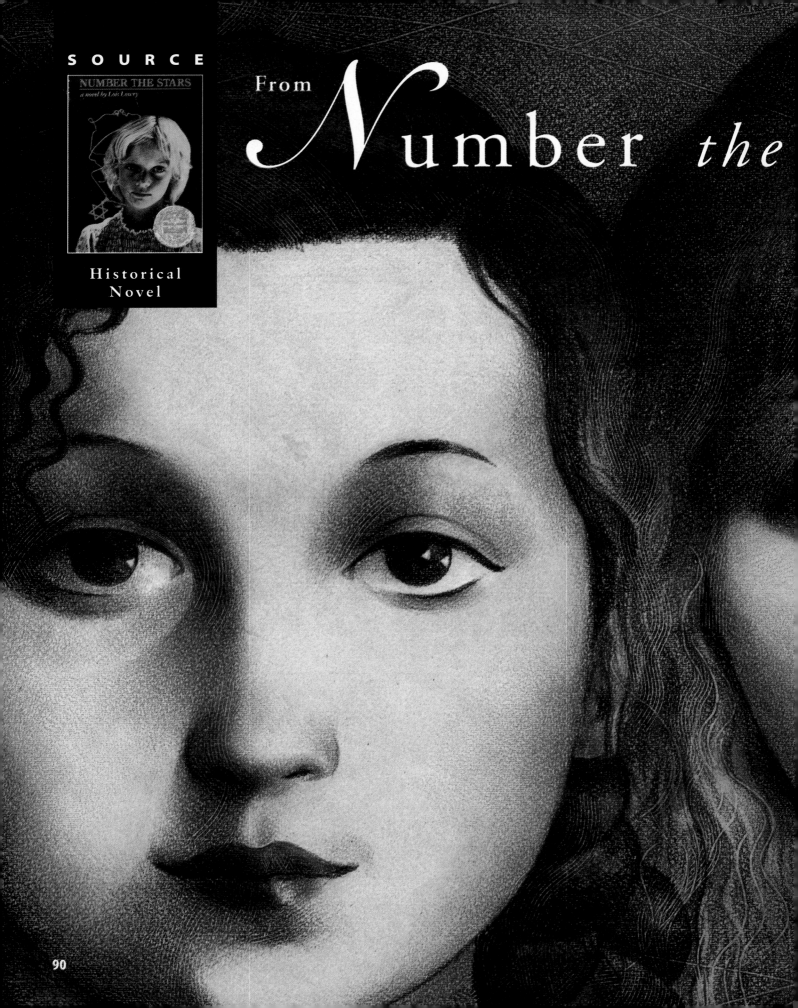

From Number the

Stars

by **Lois Lowry**
illustrated by **Raul Colon**

The year is 1943. Annemarie Johansen lives in Denmark with her father, mother, and her little sister Kirsti. Annemarie used to love her home, but now Nazi soldiers in Denmark are persecuting the country's Jews— including Annemarie's best friend, Ellen Rosen. Now Ellen's life is in danger, and Annemarie and her family must act courageously in order to save their friend.

ALONE IN THE APARTMENT while Mama was out shopping with Kirsti, Annemarie and Ellen were sprawled on the living room floor playing with paper dolls. They had cut the dolls from Mama's magazines, old ones she had saved from past years. The paper ladies had old-fashioned hair styles and clothes, and the girls had given them names from Mama's very favorite book. Mama had told Annemarie and Ellen the entire story of *Gone With the Wind*, and the girls thought it much more interesting and romantic than the king-and-queen tales that Kirsti loved.

"Come, Melanie," Annemarie said, walking her doll across the edge of the rug. "Let's dress for the ball."

"All right, Scarlett, I'm coming," Ellen replied in a sophisticated voice. She was a talented performer; she often played the leading roles in school dramatics. Games of the imagination were always fun when Ellen played.

The door opened and Kirsti stomped in, her face tear-stained and glowering. Mama followed her with an exasperated look and set a package down on the table.

"I won't!" Kirsti sputtered. "I won't ever, *ever*, wear them! Not if you chain me in a prison and beat me with sticks!"

Annemarie giggled and looked questioningly at her mother. Mrs. Johansen sighed. "I bought Kirsti some new shoes," she explained. "She's outgrown her old ones."

"Goodness, Kirsti," Ellen said, "I wish my mother would get *me* some new shoes. I love new things, and it's so hard to find them in the stores."

"Not if you go to a *fish* store!" Kirsti bellowed. "But most mothers wouldn't make their daughters wear ugly *fish* shoes!"

"Kirsten," Mama said soothingly, "you know it wasn't a fish store. And we were lucky to find shoes at all."

Kirsti sniffed. "Show them," she commanded. "Show Annemarie and Ellen how ugly they are."

Mama opened the package and took out a pair of little girl's shoes. She held them up, and Kirsti looked away in disgust.

"You know there's no leather anymore," Mama explained. "But they've found a way to make shoes out of fish skin. I don't think these are too ugly."

Annemarie and Ellen looked at the fish skin shoes. Annemarie took one in her hand and examined it. It was odd-looking; the fish scales were visible. But it was a shoe, and her sister needed shoes.

"It's not so bad, Kirsti," she said, lying a little.

Ellen turned the other one over in her hand. "You know," she said, "it's only the color that's ugly."

"Green!" Kirsti wailed. "I will never, *ever* wear green shoes!"

"In our apartment," Ellen told her, "my father has a jar of black, black ink. Would you like these shoes better if they were black?"

Kirsti frowned. "Maybe I would," she said, finally.

"Well, then," Ellen told her, "tonight, if your mama doesn't mind, I'll take the shoes home and ask my father to make them black for you, with his ink."

Mama laughed. "I think that would be a fine improvement. What do you think, Kirsti?"

Kirsti pondered. "Could he make them shiny?" she asked. "I want them shiny."

Ellen nodded. "I think he could. I think they'll be quite pretty, black and shiny."

Kirsti nodded. "All right, then," she said. "But you musn't tell anyone that they're *fish*. I don't want anyone to know." She took her new shoes, holding them disdainfully, and put them on a chair.

Then she looked with interest at the paper dolls.

"Can I play, too?" Kirsti asked. "Can I have a doll?" She squatted beside Annemarie and Ellen on the floor.

Sometimes, Annemarie thought, Kirsti was such a pest, always butting in. But the apartment was small. There was no other place for Kirsti to play. And if they told her to go away, Mama would scold.

"Here," Annemarie said, and handed her sister a cut-out little girl doll. "We're playing *Gone With the Wind*. Melanie and Scarlett are going to a ball. You can be Bonnie. She's Scarlett's daughter."

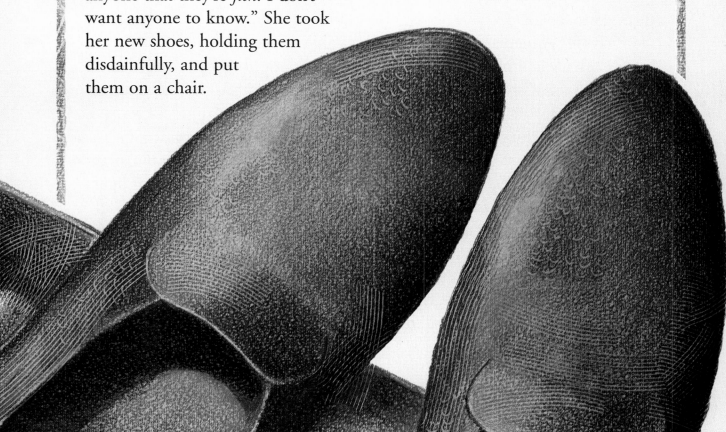

Kirsti danced her doll up and down happily. "I'm going to the ball!" she announced in a high, pretend voice.

Ellen giggled. "A little girl wouldn't go to a ball. Let's make them go someplace else. Let's make them go to Tivoli!"

"Tivoli!" Annemarie began to laugh. "That's in Copenhagen! *Gone With the Wind* is in America!"

"Tivoli, Tivoli, Tivoli," little Kirsti sang, twirling her doll in a circle.

"It doesn't matter, because it's only a game anyway," Ellen pointed out. "Tivoli can be over there, by that chair. 'Come, Scarlett,'" she said, using her doll voice, "'we shall go to Tivoli to dance and watch the fireworks, and maybe there will be some handsome men there! Bring your silly daughter Bonnie, and she can ride on the carousel.'"

Annemarie grinned and walked her Scarlett toward the chair that Ellen had designated as Tivoli. She loved Tivoli Gardens, in the heart of Copenhagen; her parents had taken her there, often, when she was a little girl. She remembered the music and brightly colored lights, the carousel and ice cream and especially the magnificent fireworks in the evenings: the huge colored splashes and bursts of lights in the evening sky.

"I remember the fireworks best of all," she commented to Ellen.

"Me too," Kirsti said. "I remember the fireworks."

"Silly," Annemarie scoffed.

"You never saw the fireworks." Tivoli Gardens was closed now. The German occupation forces had burned part of it, perhaps as a way of punishing the fun-loving Danes for their lighthearted pleasures.

Kirsti drew herself up, her small shoulders stiff. "I did too," she said belligerently. "It was my birthday. I woke up in the night and I could hear the booms. And there were lights in the sky. Mama said it was fireworks for my birthday!"

Then Annemarie remembered. Kirsti's birthday was late in August. And that night, only a month before, she, too, had been awakened and frightened by the sound of explosions. Kirsti was right—the sky in the southeast had been ablaze, and Mama had comforted her by calling it a birthday celebration. "Imagine, such fireworks for a little girl five years old!" Mama had said, sitting on their bed, holding the dark curtain aside to look through the window at the lighted sky.

The next evening's newspaper had told the sad truth. The Danes had destroyed their own naval fleet, blowing up the vessels one by one, as the Germans approached to take over the ships for their own use.

"How sad the king must be," Annemarie had heard Mama say to Papa when they read the news.

"How proud," Papa had replied.

It had made Annemarie feel sad and proud, too, to picture the tall, aging king, perhaps with tears in his blue eyes, as he looked at the remains of his small navy, which now lay submerged and broken in the harbor.

"I don't want to play anymore, Ellen," she said suddenly, and put her doll on the table.

"I have to go home, anyway," Ellen said. "I have to help Mama with the house-cleaning. Thursday is our New Year. Did you know that?"

"Why is it yours?" asked Kirsti. "Isn't it our New Year, too?"

"No. It's the Jewish New Year. That's just for us. But if you want, Kirsti, you can come that night and watch Mama light the candles."

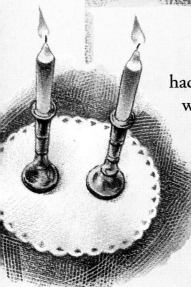

Annemarie and Kirsti had often been invited to watch Mrs. Rosen light the Sabbath candles on Friday evenings. She covered her head with a cloth and said a special prayer in Hebrew as she did so. Annemarie always stood very quietly, awed, to watch; even Kirsti, usually such a chatterbox, was always still at that time. They didn't understand the words or the meaning, but they could feel what a special time it was for the Rosens.

"Yes," Kirsti agreed happily. "I'll come and watch your mama light the candles, and I'll wear my new black shoes."

BUT THIS TIME WAS to be different. Leaving for school on Thursday with her sister, Annemarie saw the Rosens walking to the synagogue early in the morning, dressed in their best clothes. She waved to Ellen, who waved happily back.

"Lucky Ellen," Annemarie said to Kirsti. "She doesn't have to go to school today."

"But she probably has to sit very, very still, like we do in church," Kirsti pointed out. "*That's* no fun."

That afternoon, Mrs. Rosen knocked at their door but didn't come inside. Instead, she spoke for a long time in a hurried, tense voice to Annemarie's mother in the hall. When Mama returned, her face was worried, but her voice was cheerful.

"Girls," she said, "we have a nice surprise. Tonight Ellen will be coming to stay overnight and to be our guest for a few days! It isn't often we have a visitor."

Kirsti clapped her hands in delight.

"But, Mama," Annemarie said, in dismay, "it's their New Year. They were going to have a celebration at home! Ellen told me that her mother managed to get a chicken someplace, and she was going to roast it—their first roast chicken in a year or more!"

"Their plans have changed," Mama said briskly. "Mr. and Mrs. Rosen have been called away to visit some relatives. So Ellen will stay with us. Now, let's get busy and put clean sheets on your bed. Kirsti, you may sleep with Mama and Papa tonight, and we'll let the big girls giggle together by themselves."

Kirsti pouted, and it was clear that she was about to argue. "Mama will tell you a special story tonight," her mother said. "One just for you."

"About a king?" Kirsti asked dubiously.

"About a king, if you wish," Mama replied.

"All right, then. But there must be a queen, too," Kirsti said.

THOUGH MRS. ROSEN had sent her chicken to the Johansens, and Mama made a lovely dinner large enough for second helpings all around, it was not an evening of laughter and talk. Ellen was silent at dinner. She looked frightened. Mama and Papa tried to speak of cheerful things, but it was clear that they were worried, and it made Annemarie worry, too. Only Kirsti was unaware of the quiet tension in the room. Swinging her feet in their newly blackened and shiny shoes, she chattered and giggled during dinner.

"Early bedtime tonight, little one," Mama announced after the dishes were washed. "We need extra time for the long story I promised, about the king and queen." She disappeared with Kirsti into the bedroom.

"What's happening?" Annemarie asked when she and Ellen were alone with Papa in the living room. "Something's wrong. What is it?"

Papa's face was troubled. "I wish that I could protect you children from this knowledge," he said quietly. "Ellen, you already know. Now we must tell Annemarie."

He turned to her and stroked her hair with his gentle hand. "This morning, at the synagogue, the rabbi told his congregation that the Nazis have taken the synagogue lists of all the Jews. Where they live, what their names are. Of course the Rosens were on that list, along with many others."

"Why? Why did they want those names?"

"They plan to arrest all the

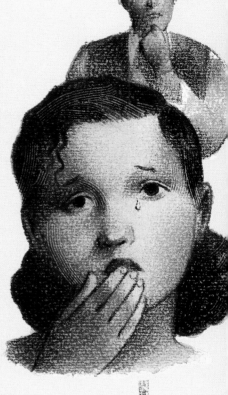

Danish Jews. They plan to take them away. And we have been told that they may come tonight."

"I don't understand! Take them where?"

Her father shook his head. "We don't know where, and we don't really know why. They call it 'relocation.' We don't even know what that means. We only know that it is wrong, and it is dangerous, and we must help."

Annemarie was stunned. She looked at Ellen and saw that her best friend was crying silently.

"Where are Ellen's parents? We must help them, too!"

"We couldn't take all three of them. If the Germans came to search our apartment, it would be clear that the Rosens were here. One person we can hide. Not three. So Peter has helped Ellen's parents to go elsewhere. We don't know where. Ellen doesn't know either. But they are safe."

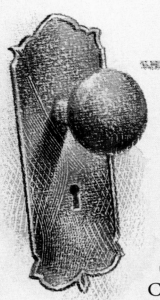

Ellen sobbed aloud, and put her face in her hands. Papa put his arm around her. "They are safe, Ellen. I promise you that. You will see them again quite soon. Can you try hard to believe my promise?"

Ellen hesitated, nodded, and wiped her eyes with her hand.

"But, Papa," Annemarie said, looking around the small apartment, with its few pieces of furniture: the fat stuffed sofa, the table and chairs, the small bookcase against the wall. "You said that we would hide her. How can we do that? Where can she hide?"

Papa smiled. "That part is easy. It will be as your mama said: you two will sleep together in your bed, and you may giggle and talk and tell secrets to each other. And if anyone comes—"

Ellen interrupted him. "Who might come? Will it be soldiers? Like the ones on the corners?" Annemarie remembered how terrified Ellen had looked the day when the soldier had questioned them on the corner.

"I really don't think anyone will. But it never hurts to be prepared. If anyone should come, even soldiers, you two will be sisters. You are together so much, it will be easy for you to pretend that you are sisters."

He rose and walked to the window. He pulled the lace curtain aside and looked down into the street. Outside, it was beginning to grow dark. Soon they would have to draw the black curtains that all Danes had on their windows; the entire city had to be completely darkened at night. In a nearby tree, a bird was singing; otherwise it was quiet. It was the last night of September.

"Go, now, and get into your nightgowns. It will be a long night."

Annemarie and Ellen got to their feet. Papa suddenly crossed the room and put his arms around them both. He kissed the top of each head: Annemarie's blond one, which reached to his shoulder, and Ellen's dark hair, the thick curls braided as always into pigtails.

"Don't be frightened," he said to them softly. "Once I had three daughters. Tonight I am proud to have three daughters again."

. . . .

"DO YOU REALLY think anyone will come?" Ellen asked nervously, turning to Annemarie in the bedroom. "Your father doesn't think so."

"Of course not. They're always threatening stuff. They just like to scare people." Annemarie took her nightgown from a hook in the closet.

"Anyway, if they did, it would give me a chance to practice acting. I'd just pretend to be Lise. I wish I were taller, though." Ellen stood on tiptoe, trying to make herself tall. She laughed at herself, and her voice was more relaxed.

"You were great as the Dark Queen in the school play last year," Annemarie told her. "You should be an actress when you grow up."

"My father wants me to be a teacher. He wants *everyone* to be a teacher, like him. But maybe I could convince him that I should go to acting school." Ellen stood on tiptoe again, and made an imperious gesture with her arm. "I am the Dark Queen," she intoned dramatically. "I have come to command the night!"

"You should try saying, 'I am Lise Johansen!'"Annemarie said, grinning. "If you told

the Nazis that you were the Dark Queen, they'd haul you off to a mental institution."

Ellen dropped her actress pose and sat down, with her legs curled under her, on the bed. "They won't really come here, do you think?" she asked again.

Annemarie shook her head. "Not in a million years." She picked up her hairbrush.

The girls found themselves whispering as they got ready for bed. There was no need, really, to whisper; they were, after all, supposed to be normal sisters, and Papa had said they could giggle and talk. The bedroom door was closed.

But the night did seem, somehow, different from a normal night. And so they whispered.

"How did your sister die, Annemarie?" Ellen asked suddenly. "I remember when it happened. And I remember the funeral—it was the only time I have ever been in a Lutheran church. But I never knew just what happened."

"I don't know *exactly*," Annemarie confessed. "She and Peter were out somewhere together, and then there was a telephone call, that there had been an accident. Mama and Papa rushed to the hospital—remember, your mother came and stayed with me and Kirsti? Kirsti was already asleep and she slept right through everything, she was so little then. But I stayed up, and I was with your mother in the living room when my parents came home in the middle of the night. And they told me Lise had died."

"I remember it was raining," Ellen said sadly. "It was still raining the next morning when Mama told me. Mama was crying, and the rain made it seem as if the whole *world* was crying."

Annemarie finished brushing her long hair and handed her hairbrush to her best friend. Ellen undid her braids, lifted her dark hair away from the thin gold chain she wore around her neck—the chain that held the Star of David— and began to brush her thick curls.

"I think it was partly because of the rain. They said she was hit by a car. I suppose the streets were slippery, and it was getting dark, and maybe the driver just couldn't see," Annemarie went on, remembering.

"Papa looked so angry. He made one hand into a fist, and he kept pounding it into the other hand. I remember the noise of it: slam, slam, slam."

Together they got into the wide bed and pulled up the covers. Annemarie blew out the candle and drew the dark curtains aside so that the open window near the bed let in some air. "See that blue trunk in the corner?" she said, pointing through the darkness. "Lots of Lise's things are there. Even her wedding dress. Mama and Papa have never looked at those things, not since the day they packed them away."

Ellen sighed. "She would have looked so beautiful in her wedding dress. She had such a pretty smile. I used to pretend that she was *my* sister, too."

"She would have liked that," Annemarie told her. "She loved you."

"That's the worst thing in the world," Ellen whispered. "To be dead so young. I wouldn't want the Germans to take my family away—to make us live someplace else. But still, it wouldn't be as bad as being dead."

Annemarie leaned over and hugged her. "They won't take you away," she said. "Not your parents, either. Papa promised that they were safe, and he always keeps his promises. And you are quite safe, here with us."

For a while they continued to murmur in the dark, but the murmurs were interrupted by yawns. Then Ellen's voice stopped, she turned over, and in a minute her breathing was quiet and slow.

Annemarie stared at the window where the sky was outlined and a tree branch moved slightly in the breeze. Everything seemed very familiar, very comforting. Dangers were no more than odd imaginings, like ghost stories that children made up to frighten one another: things that couldn't possibly happen. Annemarie felt completely safe here in her own home, with her parents in the next room and her best friend asleep beside her. She yawned contentedly and closed her eyes.

It was hours later, but still dark, when she was awakened abruptly by the pounding on the apartment door.

ANNEMARIE EASED THE bedroom door open quietly, only a crack, and peeked out. Behind her, Ellen was sitting up, her eyes wide.

She could see Mama and Papa in their nightclothes, moving about. Mama held a lighted candle, but as Annemarie watched, she went to a lamp and switched it on. It was so long a time since they had dared to use the strictly rationed electricity after dark that the light in the room seemed startling to Annemarie, watching through the slightly opened bedroom door. She saw her mother look automatically to the blackout curtains, making sure that they were tightly drawn.

Papa opened the front door to the soldiers.

"This is the Johansen apartment?" A deep voiced asked the question loudly, in the terribly accented Danish.

"Our name is on the door, and I see you have a flashlight," Papa answered. "What do you want? Is something wrong?"

"I understand you are a friend of your neighbors the Rosens, Mrs. Johansen," the soldier said angrily.

"Sophy Rosen is my friend, that is true," Mama said quietly. "Please, could you speak more softly? My children are asleep."

"Then you will be so kind as to tell me where the Rosens are." He made no effort to lower his voice.

"I assume they are at home, sleeping. It is four in the morning, after all," Mama said.

Annemarie heard the soldier stalk across the living room toward the kitchen. From her hiding place in the narrow sliver of an open doorway, she could see the heavy uniformed man, a holstered pistol at his waist, in the entrance to the kitchen, peering in toward the sink.

Another German voice said, "The Rosens' apartment is empty. We are wondering if they might be visiting their good friends the Johansens."

"Well," said Papa, moving slightly so that he was standing in front of Annemarie's bedroom door, and she could see nothing except the dark blur of his back, "as you see, you are mistaken. There is no one here but my family."

"You will not object if we look around." The voice was harsh, and it was not a question.

"It seems we have no choice," Papa replied.

"Please don't wake my children," Mama requested again. "There is no need to frighten little ones."

The heavy, booted feet moved across the floor again and into the other bedroom. A closet door opened and closed with a bang.

Annemarie eased her bedroom door closed silently. She stumbled through the darkness to the bed.

"Ellen," she whispered urgently, "take your necklace off!"

Ellen's hands flew to her neck. Desperately she began trying to unhook the tiny clasp. Outside the bedroom door, the harsh voices and heavy footsteps continued.

"I can't get it open!" Ellen said frantically. "I never take it off—I can't even remember how to open it!"

Annemarie heard a voice just outside the door. "What is here?"

"Shhh," her mother replied. "My daughters' bedroom. They are sound asleep."

"Hold still," Annemarie commanded. "This will hurt." She grabbed the little gold chain, yanked with all her strength, and broke it. As the door opened and light flooded into the bedroom, she crumpled it into her hand and closed her fingers tightly.

Terrified, both girls looked up at the three Nazi officers who entered the room.

One of the men aimed a flashlight around the bedroom. He went to the closet and looked inside. Then with a sweep of his gloved hand he pushed to the floor several coats and a bathrobe that hung from pegs on the wall.

There was nothing else in the room except a chest of drawers, the blue decorated trunk in the corner, and a heap of Kirsti's dolls piled in a small rocking chair. The flashlight beam touched each thing in turn. Angrily the officer turned toward the bed.

"Get up!" he ordered. "Come out here!"

Trembling, the two girls rose from the bed and followed him, brushing past the two remaining officers in the doorway, to the living room.

Annemarie looked around. These three uniformed men were different from the ones on the street corners. The street soldiers were often young, sometimes ill at ease, and Annemarie remembered how the Giraffe had, for a moment, let his harsh pose slip and had smiled at Kirsti.

But these men were older and their faces were set with anger.

Her parents were standing beside each other, their faces tense, but Kirsti was nowhere in sight. Thank goodness that Kirsti slept through almost anything. If they had wakened her, she would be wailing—or worse, she would be angry, and her fists would fly.

"Your names?" the officer barked.

"Annemarie Johansen. And this is my sister—"

"Quiet! Let her speak for herself. Your name?" He was glaring at Ellen.

Ellen swallowed. "Lise," she said, and cleared her throat. "Lise Johansen."

The officer stared at them grimly.

"Now," Mama said in a strong voice, "you have seen that we are not hiding anything. May my children go back to bed?"

The officer ignored her. Suddenly he grabbed a handful of Ellen's hair. Ellen winced.

He laughed scornfully. "You have a blond child sleeping in the other room. And you have this blond daughter—" He gestured toward Annemarie with his head. "Where did you get the dark-haired one?" He twisted the lock of Ellen's hair. "From a different father? From the milkman?"

Papa stepped forward. "Don't speak to my wife in such a way. Let go of my daughter or I will report you for such treatment."

"Or maybe you got her some-place else?" the officer continued with a sneer. "From the Rosens?"

For a moment no one spoke. Then Annemarie, watching in panic, saw her father move swiftly to the small bookcase and take out a book. She saw that he was holding the family photograph album. Very quickly he searched through its pages, found what he was looking for, and tore out three pictures from three separate pages.

He handed them to the German officer, who released Ellen's hair.

"You will see each of my daughters, each with her name written on the photograph," Papa said.

Annemarie knew instantly which photographs he had chosen. The album had many snapshots—all the poorly focused pictures of school events and birthday parties. But it also contained a portrait, taken by a photographer, of each girl as a tiny infant. Mama had written in her delicate handwriting, the name of each baby daughter across the bottom of those photographs.

She realized too, with an icy feeling, why Papa had torn them from the book. At the bottom of each page, below the photograph

itself, was written the date. And the real Lise Johansen had been born twenty-one years earlier.

"Kirsten Elisabeth," the officer read, looking at Kirsti's baby picture. He let the photograph fall to the floor.

"Annemarie," he read next, glanced at her, and dropped the second photograph.

"Lise Margrete," he read finally, and stared at Ellen for a long, unwavering moment. In her mind, Annemarie pictured the photograph that he held: the baby, wide-eyed, propped against a pillow, her tiny hand holding a silver teething ring, her bare feet visible below the hem of an embroidered dress. The wispy curls. Dark.

The officer tore the photograph in half and dropped the pieces on the floor. Then he turned, the heels of his shiny boots grinding into the pictures, and left the apartment. Without a word, the other two officers followed. Papa stepped forward and closed the door behind him.

Annemarie relaxed the clenched fingers of her right hand, which still clutched Ellen's necklace. She looked down, and saw that she had imprinted the Star of David into her palm.

RESCUE:
THE DANISH BOAT

Millions of people lost their lives in the Holocaust. Some were lucky enough to be saved—because of the courage of a few people who acted heroically during a time of crisis.

On April 26, 1993, the United States Holocaust Memorial Museum in Washington, D.C., opened so that the stories of the victims wouldn't be forgotten. The poster on the next page, designed by the United States Holocaust Memorial Council, is a testimony to the people of Denmark who helped Jews escape from their country into safety.

The background of the poster is a nautical map showing the Oresund, the body of water between Denmark and Sweden. The boat pictured in the poster is a Danish motorboat built in the 1930s or 1940s. Courageous Danes used these small wooden boats to smuggle nearly 7,000 Danish Jews across the Oresund to safety in Sweden. The black and white photograph at the bottom of the poster shows a small group of Danish citizens making their way across the sea to neighboring Sweden. These men and women probably included members of the Resistance, an underground movement that planned the secret operations to rescue the Jews. Many brave young Resistance leaders sacrificed their own lives to help save their compatriots.

The United States Holocaust Memorial Museum in Washington, D.C.

Right: Poster from the United States Holocaust Memorial Museum

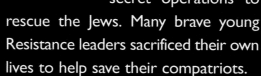

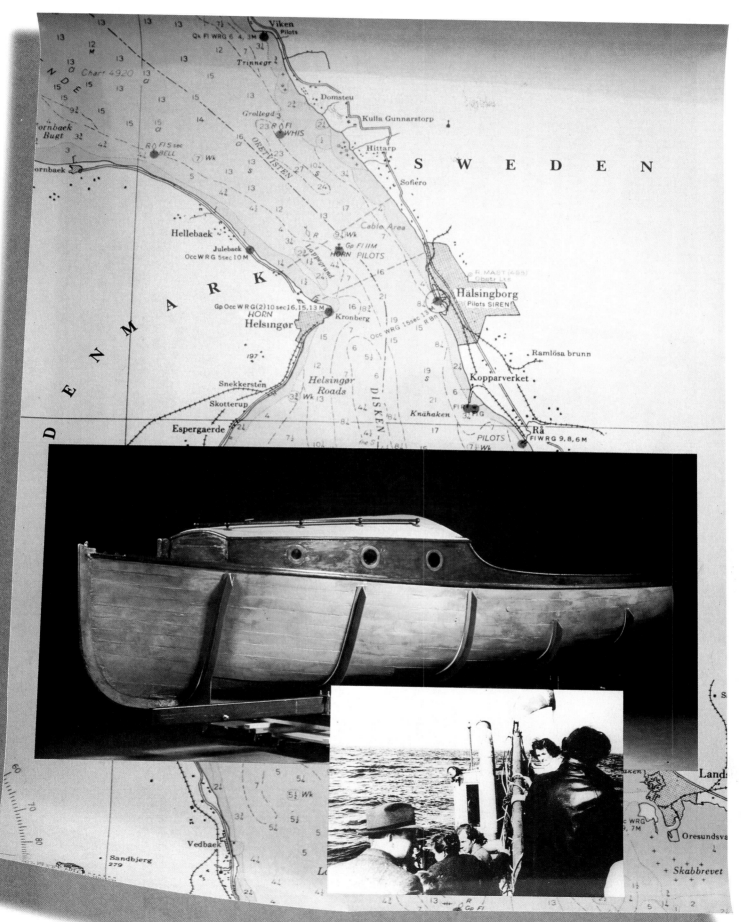

How to Write a Tribute

Demonstrate *your* appreciation of someone who *inspires* you!

Inspirations can come from many sources. The accomplishments of friends and family members can be inspirational, as can the achievements of famous people. One way to show respect for someone who has inspired you is to write a tribute to that person. A tribute contains biographical facts, stories, and personal feelings about the subject, as well as things the person has said. Tributes come in many forms. Some common ones are poems, songs, and speeches.

Jane Goodall

Brainstorm

Choose a subject for your tribute. The subject can be a friend or relative, or someone else whom you know well. You could also write a tribute to a celebrity or some other inspiring individual whom you don't know personally.

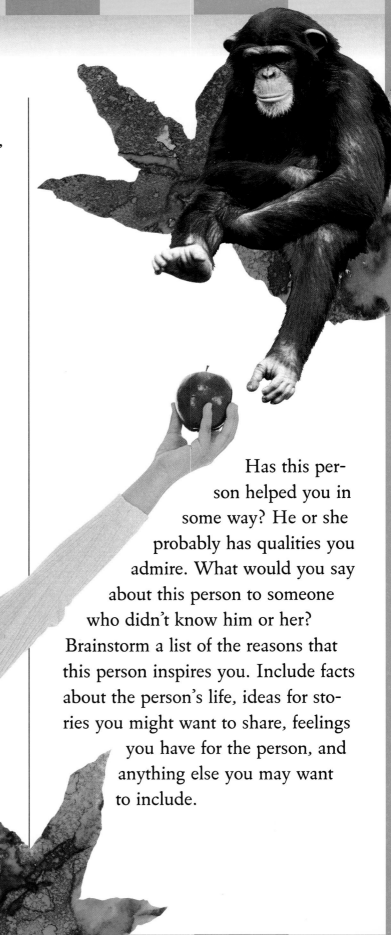

TOOLS

- paper and pencil
- research materials

Before you begin to write, you have to think about what you'd like to say about your subject.

Has this person helped you in some way? He or she probably has qualities you admire. What would you say about this person to someone who didn't know him or her? Brainstorm a list of the reasons that this person inspires you. Include facts about the person's life, ideas for stories you might want to share, feelings you have for the person, and anything else you may want to include.

2 Choose a Format

After you have decided what you want to say about your subject, you'll need to choose a style for your tribute. The style of your tribute should reflect those things that make your subject special. For example, if you are paying tribute to a musician, you may want to write a song.

Select the format that works best for you. You can create your own, or choose one from the following:

- a poem
- music video
- a play
- a speech
- a book jacket
- a collage

3 Research Your Subject

Before you begin writing your tribute, you'll need some basic information about your subject, such as where and when the person was born, and what he or she does for a living. If you chose the same person you used for your biographical sketch, then you probably already have a lot of this information.

You will also want to personalize your tribute. In addition to sharing your own feelings, comments, and stories about the subject, you may want to collect those of other people.

If your subject is a celebrity, you may need to get your information from books, magazines, newspapers, or videos. Try to find out how your subject became the type of person who inspires you.

Tip Include unique items, such as lyrics from your subject's favorite song or pictures of his or her birthplace or current home, to make your tribute more interesting.

How Am I Doing?

Before you put your tribute together, take a minute to ask yourself these questions:

● Did I find enough information about my subject?

● Did I think about how this person has made a difference in my life?

● Did I gather a good mix of facts and feelings for the tribute?

4 Write Your Tribute

How will you present the information you've gathered? That will depend on the format you've chosen. If you are writing a poem, for example, you might want to think about how many stanzas it should have and whether it will rhyme. If you are giving a speech, you might want to select a funny quote or an amusing story for your introduction. Remember that you do not have to use all of your information—include whatever is most interesting and important.

If You Are Using a Computer ...

Create your tribute in the Newsletter format on your computer. Write a headline telling just how special your subject is. Use clip art to illustrate the tribute.

5 Present Your Tribute

The format you have chosen will also influence the type of presentation you make. If you wrote a song, for instance, you will probably want to perform it. If you wrote a poem, you might want to make a collage and put your poem in the center. You and your classmates might want to organize a "Tribute Ceremony," and take turns presenting your tributes. If possible, arrange for some of the honorees to attend!

CONGRATULATIONS

An important part of knowing yourself is getting to know the people who are important to you. Maybe you will inspire someone yourself!

Joseph Shabalala
Musician

Glossary

am·pli·fies
(am′plə fīs) *verb*
Increases in power or
volume; makes louder.
▲ **amplify**

an·dan·te
(än dän′ tā) *adverb*
Music played in a
moderately slow tempo.

bat·ting av·er·age
(bat′ing av′ ər ij) *noun*
A measure of a player's
hitting ability.

bird·seed
(bûrd′sēd′) *noun*
Seeds or mixtures of seeds
used as food for birds.

cel·lo
(chel′ō) *noun*
A musical instrument that
looks like a large violin.
When it is played, a cello
is held between the knees
with one end on the floor.

cham·ber group
(chām′bər grōōp′) *noun*
A group of between two
and nine musicians playing
string or wind instruments.

con·serv·a·to·ry
(kən sûr′və tôr′ ē) *noun*
A school where music is
studied.

coo·ing
(kōō′ing) *verb*
Making a soft, murmuring
sound like that of doves and
pigeons. ▲ **coo**

dream (drēm) *noun*
Thought, feeling, or experi-
ence occurring during sleep.

dug·out (dug′out′) *noun*
A place where baseball
players sit during a game
when they are not on the
field. Dugouts are usually
built below ground at the
side of a baseball field.

dugout

ex•plain•ing
(ĭk splān′ing) *verb*
Showing the meaning of something. The teacher told the class to wait until he was finished *explaining* the lesson before asking questions. ▲ **explain**

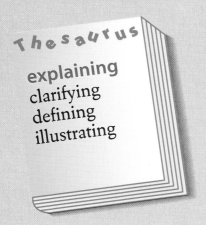

Thesaurus

explaining
clarifying
defining
illustrating

flut•tered (flŭt′ərd) *verb*
Flapped very quickly.
▲ **flutter**

foul (foul) *noun*
A baseball hit out of fair play.

ground•ers
(groun′dərs) *noun*
Baseballs that roll or bounce along the ground when hit; also called ground balls. ▲ **grounder**

hom•ers
(hō′mərz) *noun*
Hits in baseball that allow batters to go around all the bases and score a run; also called home runs.
▲ **homer**

in•ning (in′ing) *noun*
A part of a baseball game in which each team is at bat once and in the field once. There are usually nine innings in a baseball game. During an inning, each team has a chance to score until three outs are made against it.

main tun•ing slide
(mān tōōn′ing slīd) *noun*
The tube on a trumpet that is adjusted to tune the instrument.

mem•o•ry
(mem′ə rē) *noun*
Something that is remembered; a recollection.

mouth•piece
(mouth′pēs′) *noun*
A piece or part of a musical instrument that is placed between or near the lips.

Na•zi (nät′sē) *noun*
A member of the National Socialist German Workers' Party which controlled Germany from 1933 to 1945.

a	add	ŏŏ	took	ə =
ā	ace	ōō	pool	a in *above*
â	care	u	up	e in *sicken*
ä	palm	û	burn	i in *possible*
e	end	yōō	fuse	o in *melon*
ē	equal	oi	oil	u in *circus*
i	it	ou	pout	
ī	ice	ng	ring	
o	odd	th	thin	
ō	open	ŧh	this	
ô	order	zh	vision	

Glossary

oc·cu·pa·tion forces
(ok´yə pā´shən fôrcs)
noun
Military forces that control a foreign territory.
▲ occupation force

out·field·er
(out´fēl´d ər) *noun*
A baseball player who plays in the area beyond the diamond.

per·se·cut·ing
(pûr´si kyōōt´ing) *verb*
Treating in an unjustifiably cruel or harsh way, often because of religion or race.
▲ persecute

Thesaurus

persecuting
harassing
badgering
tormenting

per·fect pitch
(pûr´fikt pich) *noun*
The ability to identify a note upon hearing it.

pi·geon
(pij´ən) *noun*
A kind of bird; slang for someone who is easily taken advantage of.

pres·to
(pres´tō) *noun*
Music played at a fast tempo.

ra·tioned
(rash´ənd) *verb*
Limited the supply of. During the war, the government *rationed* oil.
▲ ration

Thesaurus

rationed
apportioned
distributed
parceled out

re·lo·ca·tion
(rē´lō ka´shən) *noun*
The process of moving someone or something from one place to another.

scales (skālz) *noun*
A group of musical notes going up or down in pitch at fixed intervals. Most musical scales are made up of eight notes.
▲ scale

Word History

The noun **scale** has several other meanings. It can mean:
- a device for weighing
- a series of marks laid down at determinate distances for purposes of measurement
- one of the horny flattened structures that covers the skin of a fish.

spi·raled (spī´rəld) *verb*
Followed a circular path.
▲ spiral

sta·di·um
(stā´dē əm) *noun*
A sports arena; a structure, usually oval or horseshoe-shaped, containing rows of seats where people sit to watch sporting events. Wrigley Field is a famous *stadium* located in Chicago.

trumpet

vi•bra•to
(vi brä′tō) *noun*
A musical effect created by slightly and quickly changing pitch. It results in a pulsating effect that sounds like a single pitch.

Word History

Vibrato is based on the word *vibrate*. It comes from a Latin word meaning "to move back and forth quickly."

vi•sion
(vizh′ən) *noun*
Something that is imagined or seen, as in a dream. I had a *vision* of becoming a famous musician.

trum•pet
(trum′pit) *noun*
A brass wind instrument made up of a long coiled tube with a flared end.

Fact File

The oldest **trumpet** that has been discovered is a bronze trumpet found in Egypt. It dates from the 2nd millenium B.C.

valves (valvz) *noun*
Devices that stop or control the flow of a liquid, air, or gas through a pipe or other passageway. Your trumpet would sound better if you cleaned out the *valves*. ▲ **valve**

vet•er•i•nar•i•ans
(vet′ər ə när′ē anz) *noun*
Animal doctors.
▲ **veterinarian**

a	add	o͝o	took	ə =
ā	ace	o͞o	pool	a in *above*
â	care	u	up	e in *sicken*
ä	palm	û	burn	i in *possible*
e	end	yo͞o	fuse	o in *melon*
ē	equal	oi	oil	u in *circus*
i	it	ou	pout	
ī	ice	ng	ring	
o	odd	th	thin	
ō	open	th	this	
ô	order	zh	vision	

Authors & Illustrators

Joseph Bruchac *pages 10–27*
Joseph Bruchac loves being a writer and storyteller. He says that his work has allowed him to travel all over the United States, to live in Africa, and to meet interesting people wherever he goes. When he was small, his Abenaki grandfather taught him how to walk quietly in the woods and how to fish. His grandmother encouraged his love of reading. *Fox Song* was inspired by his own family stories and his own feelings about how important a grandparent can be in a child's life.

Raul Colon *pages 90–111*
As a child, this artist suffered from severe asthma. While his friends were out playing, he sat indoors filling stacks of notebooks with drawings. Now he earns his living drawing in his trademark style, using watercolors and pencils to create scratches that add texture to his art. Raul Colon also does careful research to prepare for each project. In the library, he found photographs of children from World War II who became the models for his illustrations for *Number the Stars*.

Floyd Cooper *pages 80–85*

This award-winning artist began his career working on greeting cards and advertising campaigns, but he wanted to find another outlet for his talent. Now he's happiest when he's working on children's books. Not only is he doing something he loves, but he also is doing something he considers quite important. Floyd Cooper believes that children are on the front lines in improving society and that's one reason they deserve the best books possible.

"My personal goal is to take the reader on a journey into the story."

Jill Krementz *pages 62–69*

Several years ago, journalist Jill Krementz took some pictures of a young family friend who was studying ballet. She photographed the girl as she practiced and performed. These photographs were the start of a book called *A Very Young Dancer*. This book was the first title in the now popular series that profiles the skill and determination of young performers. Each title in the series meant that the author spent lots of time with the subject of the book. Each book also led to another friendship—Jill Krementz keeps in touch with the children from all of her books!

Lois Lowry *pages 90–111*

When her friend Annelise Platt told her about life in Denmark during the German occupation, the character of Annemarie Johansen began to take shape in Lois Lowry's imagination. Then, as she does for every book she writes, this author began combining scenes and dialogue, until she had created the story she wanted to tell. She says that for her writing a book is like making a patchwork quilt—it is filled with colorful pieces that join together to make a meaningful whole.

Books &

Author Study

More by Patricia MacLachlan

Arthur, for the Very First Time
Arthur's summer with his aunt and uncle gives him new pride, and a new way to look at himself and his world.

Baby
When a family takes in an abandoned baby, everyone's life changes for the better.

Skylark
In this sequel to the popular *Sarah, Plain and Tall*, Sarah and her new family find that a drought threatens their home.

Patricia MacLachlan

Fiction

Bridge to Terabithia
by Katherine Paterson
Jesse is shy and uncertain about where he fits in. Then one day a girl named Leslie joins his fifth grade class, and soon Jesse's life changes forever.

Me, Mop, and the Moondance Kid
by Walter Dean Myers
In this fast and funny novel, T.J., his younger brother, and their friend Olivia help each other fulfill their dreams—both on and off the baseball field.

The Secret Garden
by Frances Hodgson Burnett
This classic children's story tells of Mary Lennox and her ailing cousin, who find that the unhappiness in their lives fades away as they work together to restore a neglected garden.

Nonfiction

Champions: Stories of Ten Remarkable Athletes
by Bill Littlefield
illustrated by Bernie Fuchs
Athletes such as Roberto Clemente, Nate "Tiny" Archibald, and Diana Golden did more than succeed at their sports. They focused on goals and overcame obstacles to reach them.

Childtimes: A Three Generation Memoir
by Eloise Greenfield and Lessie Jones Little
As they recount childhood stories, the authors celebrate the love and support they got from family members during good times and bad.

xMedia

Videos

Beethoven Lives Upstairs
The Children's Group

When the great composer Beethoven moves into Christoph's house, he turns life upside-down for everyone. But then Christoph finds a way to make friends with the new boarder and learns to appreciate both the man and his music. (52 minutes)

The Mighty Pawns
Public Media

Based on a true story, this WonderWorks video tells about a group of city kids who form a champion chess team after a teacher convinces them that using their intelligence to compete is better than fighting. (55 minutes)

Software

Famous Faces
Jasmine Multimedia Publishing
(Macintosh CD-ROM)

Meet men and women who changed history. Film footage and biographies help bring to life some of the most influential people of the twentieth century.

Melody Shop
Scholastic Inc.
(Apple)

Have you been inspired to create music? Here's a new way to compose your own songs and play them back on the computer.

Magazines

Sports Illustrated for Kids
Time, Inc.

If you want to know more about your favorite sports heroes, this monthly magazine has what you're looking for—and more.

Stone Soup
Children's Art Foundation

Have you ever thought about sharing your own poems or stories with others? This magazine publishes original work by children.

A Place to Write

Greystone International Jazz Museum
1521 Broadway
Detroit, MI 48226

Write to this museum if you would like to learn about the history of jazz and the work of great jazz musicians.

Acknowledgments

Grateful acknowledgment is made to the following sources for permission to reprint from previously published material. The publisher has made diligent efforts to trace the ownership of all copyrighted material in this volume and believes that all necessary permissions have been secured. If any errors or omissions have inadvertently been made, proper corrections will gladly be made in future editions.

Cover: Elizabeth Sayles.

Interior: "Fox Song" from FOX SONG and cover by Joseph Bruchac, illustrated by Paul Morin. Text copyright © 1993 by Joseph Bruchac, illustrations copyright © 1993 by Paul Morin. Reprinted by permission of Philomel Books.

"Gifts" by Michelle Whatoname, illustrations, and cover from RISING VOICES: WRITINGS OF YOUNG NATIVE AMERICANS selected by Arlene B. Hirschfelder and Beverly R. Singer. Copyright © 1992 by Arlene B. Hirschfelder and Beverly R. Singer. Published by Atheneum Books for Young Readers, Simon & Schuster Children's Publishing Division. Used by permission. "Gifts" was originally published in 1985 in THE EVE OF A WHITE DOVE, a collection of student poems from the Havasupai Elementary School in Arizona, edited by Mick Fedello.

"Like Father, Like Son: The Griffeys" and cover from THE MACMILLAN BOOK OF BASEBALL STORIES by Terry Egan, Stan Friedmann, and Mike Levine. Text copyright © 1992 by Terry Egan, Stan Friedmann, and Mike Levine. Reprinted by arrangement with Simon & Schuster Books for Young Readers, Simon & Schuster Children's Publishing Division. Cover illustration copyright © 1992 by Steven Petruccio. Cover reprinted by permission of Evelyne Johnson Associates.

Photographs by Walter Wick from I SPY: A PICTURE BOOK OF RIDDLES by Jean Marzollo. Illustrations and photography copyright © 1992 by Walter Wick. Published by Scholastic Inc. Used by permission. I SPY is a registered trademark of Scholastic Inc.

Selection and cover from THE FACTS AND FICTIONS OF MINNA PRATT by Patricia MacLachlan. Copyright © 1988 by Patricia MacLachlan. Reprinted by permission of HarperCollins Publishers.

Selection and cover from A VERY YOUNG MUSICIAN by Jill Krementz. Copyright © 1991 by Jill Krementz. Reprinted by permission of Simon & Schuster Books for Young Readers, Simon & Schuster Children's Publishing Division.

Use of the Robert Neumayer biographical card by permission of Achilles Track Club. Chemical Bank logo used by permission of the Chemical Bank.

"Just a Pigeon" by Dennis Fradin and cover from TRIPLE ACTION SHORT STORIES, edited by Jeri Schapiro.

Text copyright © Dennis Fradin, reprinted by permission of the author. Cover illustration by Robert Burger. Illustration copyright © 1979 by Scholastic Inc. All rights reserved. Reprinted with permission.

"Just Do It" and logo from Newsweek, March 29, 1993. Copyright © 1993, Newsweek, Inc. All rights reserved. Reprinted by permission.

Selection and cover from NUMBER THE STARS by Lois Lowry. Text copyright © 1989 by Lois Lowry. Reprinted by permission of Houghton Mifflin Co. All rights reserved. Book cover copyright © 1990 by Dell Publishing, a division of Bantam Doubleday Dell Publishing Group, Inc. Reprinted by permission. The trademarks Dell® and Yearling® are registered in the U. S. Patent and Trademark Office.

Cover from ANNE FRANK: BEYOND THE DIARY by Ruud van der Rol and Rian Verhoeven for the Anne Frank House, photograph by Anne Frank Stichting. Photograph copyright © 1992 by Anne Frank Stichting. Published by Viking, a division of Penguin Books USA Inc.

Cover from CIRCLE OF GOLD by Candy Dawson Boyd, illustrated by Charles Lilly. Illustration copyright © 1984 by Charles Lilly. Published by Scholastic Inc.

Cover from DEAR MR. HENSHAW by Beverly Cleary, illustrated by Paul O. Zelinsky. Illustration copyright © 1983 by Paul O. Zelinsky. Published by William Morrow & Company, Inc.

Cover from RACING THE SUN by Paul Pitts, illustrated by Leonid. Illustration copyright © 1988 by Leonid. Published by Avon Books, a division of The Hearst Corporation.

Photography and Illustration Credits

Photos: © John Lei for Scholastic Inc., all Tool Box items unless otherwise noted. p. 2 bl, cl, tl: © Karen Furth for Scholastic Inc. pp. 2-3: © Jack Vartoogian for Scholastic Inc. p. 3 background: © Jack Vartoogian for Scholastic Inc.; tc: © Chase Swift/Westlight. p. 4 tc: © Michael Newman/PhotoEdit; c: © Chase Swift/Westlight. p. 5 tc: © Michael Newman/PhotoEdit; c: © Chase Swift/Westlight. p. 6 tc: © Michael Newman/PhotoEdit; tc: © Chase Swift/Westlight. pp. 28-30 all baseballs: © Bob Lorenz for Scholastic Inc. pp. 28-29 background: © Comstock, Inc.; Ken Griffey Jr. & Sr.: © Ken Levine/AllSport. p. 30 c: © Focus on Sports Ken Griffey, Sr. pp. 30-31 background: © Peter Gridley/FPG International Corp. p. 31 baseballs: © Bob Lorenz for Scholastic Inc.; cr: © Brian Masck/All Sport; br: © Walter Looss, Jr./Sports Illustrated. p. 32 baseballs: © Bob Lorenz for Scholastic Inc.; all others: © Focus on Sports. p. 32 tl: Ken Griffey, Jr.: Focus on Sport; bl: Ken Griffey, Jr. & Sr.: Focus on Sport; pp. 32-33 background: © Peter Gridley/FPG International Corp. p. 33 baseballs: © Bob Lorenz for Scholastic Inc.; all others: © Focus on Sports. pp. 34-35 background: © Peter Gridley/FPG International Corp. p. 34 baseballs: © Bob Lorenz for Scholastic Inc.; cr: © Focus on Sports. p. 35 baseballs: © Bob Lorenz for Scholastic Inc.; cr: © Comstock Inc. pp. 38-39 Walter Wick for Scholastic Inc. p. 40 bl: © Jose L. Pelaez for Scholastic Inc.; br: © Stanley Bach for Scholastic Inc. p. 41 tl: © John Lei for Scholastic Inc.; br: © Jack Vartoogian for Scholastic Inc. p. 70 tc: © Ana Esperanza Nance for Scholastic Inc.; bl: © Tria Giovan/Retna Ladysmith; tl, cl: © Jack Vartoogian; tc: © Chase Swift/Westlight. pp. 70-71c: © Jack Vartoogian for Scholastic Inc. p. 71 cr: © Karen Furth for Scholastic Inc. p. 72 bl: © Jack Vartoogian for Scholastic Inc.; br: © Karen Furth for Scholastic Inc. p. 73 cr: © Jack Vartoogian for Scholastic Inc.; tl, bl: © Karen Furth for Scholastic Inc.; p. 75 tr: courtesy Achilles Track Club. p. 76 bl: © AP/Wide World Photos; br: © Stanley Bach for Scholastic Inc.; bl: UPI/Bettman. p. 77 br: © Jack Vartoogian for Scholastic Inc. p. 92 c: © Katherine Lambert. p. 93 tl: © Ted Wood/Black Star; tr: © Ben Van Hook/Black Star. p. 94 tl: © James D. Wilson/Gamm Liaison International; tr: © Marteaz A. Cyars. p. 95 tl: © James D. Wilson/Gamma Liaison International; tr: © Janice Rubin/Black Star; br: © Rob Nelson/Black Star. p. 112 c: courtesy of the U.S. Memorial Holocaust Museum. p. 113 br, bc: courtesy of the U.S. Memorial Holocaust Museum; c: courtesy of the U.S. Memorial Holocaust Museum/© Bie Bostrom for Scholastic Inc. p. 114 bl: © Kennan Ward/Bruce Coleman, Inc. p. 115 c: © C. S. Perkins/Magnum Photos, Inc.; bc: © Wolfgang Bayer. p. 116 tr: © John Chellman/Animals Animals; bl: © Stanley Bach for Scholastic Inc. p. 117 c: © C. S Perkins/Magnum Photos, Inc. p. 117 br: © Michael Nichols/Magnum Photos. p. 118 br: AP/Wide World Photos; tr: © Stanley Bach for Scholastic Inc. p. 119 br: © Jack Vartoogian for Scholastic Inc. p. 119 bl: AP/Wide World Photos. p. 120 cr: © Tom Stewart/The Stock Market. p. 123 bl: © Ana Esperanza Nance for Scholastic Inc.; tc: © UPI/Bettmann. p. 124 tl: © Carol Bruchac. p. 125 tr: courtesy Scholastic Photo Library; cr: © Bantam Doubleday Dell. p. 126 bl: © courtesy Patricia MacLachlan. p. 127 br: © Stanley Bach for Scholastic Inc.; cr: © Lori Adamski Peek/Tony Stone Worldwide.

Illustrations: pp. 8-9, 42-43, 78-79: Elizabeth Sayles; pp. 32-37: Michelle LaPorte; pp. 44-61: Rollin McGrail; pp. 62-69: Sandra Bruce; pp. 80-85: Floyd Cooper; pp. 90-111: Raul Colon.